BRITISH HUSSAR REGIMENTS 1805-1914

A. H. Bowling

ALMARK PUBLISHING CO. LTD., LONDON

First published — August 1972

ISBN 0 85524 080 6 (hard cover edition)
ISBN 0 85524 081 4 (paper covered edition)

By the same author:
SCOTTISH REGIMENTS, 1660-1914
BRITISH INFANTRY REGIMENTS, 1660-1914
INDIAN CAVALRY REGIMENTS, 1880-1914
THE FOOT GUARDS REGIMENTS, 1880-1914

Printed in Great Britain by
Vale Press Ltd., Mitcham, Surrey, CR4 4HR
for the publishers, Almark Publishing Co. Ltd.,
270 Burlington Road, New Malden,
Surrey, KT3 4NL, England

Introduction

REGIMENTS of Hussars had been fashionable in the continental armies for many years before they were introduced into the British army. This form of cavalry is mentioned in the Polish army as early as 1683, and in the French armed forces in 1692. The Prussian and Russian armies had Hussar regiments by 1721 and 1740 respectively. The interesting point about the clothing of these early hussar regiments is the way in which all countries copied each other so that articles like the fur head-dress. Mirleton, laced jacket and pelisse and the sabretache were common to all armies. By studying early prints and paintings it seems that these articles of clothing and equipment all began as a common form of everyday garment which gradually became much more elaborate with the growth of this arm of cavalry. The fur head-dress with the coloured bag is shown as being originally a coloured cloth cap with an edging of fur while the pelisse is shown as being a complete animal skin, in one picture this is shown as being a complete wolf skin. The sabretache originally served as a purse or pocket as the word 'tasche' suggests. By 1740 all of these articles had become regulated and had taken the form by which they are now known.

Although Hussars are mentioned as early as 1683 in the Polish army they never formed a great part of the cavalry, as the main strength of the Polish cavalry was its Lancer regiments. With the other great European armies—Austria-Hungary, France, Prussia and Russia—the Hussar regiments always formed part of the regular cavalry and by the time that the British had begun converting Light Dragoon regiments into Hussars the number of these regiments had increased by 1812 in the Austria-Hungary army to twelve. There were eleven in the French Army by 1812, ten in the Prussian army by 1806 and in the Russian army which had eight regiments in 1806, the number had increased to eleven by 1813. A feature of the continental regiments was the great variety of colours used in the clothing and horse furniture.

Although the British army was the last of the great powers to introduce regiments of Hussars into the cavalry it took only twenty years before these regiments were the most expensively dressed and equipped of all European cavalry regiments.

For convenience the text of this book has been divided into two parts; the first part covers the period from the introduction of Hussar clothing up to the Crimean War, the period during which the jacket and pelisse were worn. The second part covers the period until 1914, during which the tunic was worn in full dress. The text throughout the book covers the regiments only during the time that they wore Hussar clothing and appointments. Many of the detail drawings have been made from the actual items and a number of drawings are based on sketches made by military tailors. Most of the original sketches on

3

ABOVE: Regimental badges of the Hussar regiments as in 1914.

which these clothing items are based were made between 1880 and 1900. On the original drawings are many notes referring to details and some give the officer's name and the date that the garment was ordered. The drawings were used by tailors working on these garments as aids for positioning the lace and braid.

The photographs used to illustrate this book appeared originally in the *Navy and Army Gazette,* and are from the author's collection.

FRONT COVER: This photograph showing the Sergeant Major and a Staff Sergeant Farrier of the 13th Hussars was published as a postcard over 70 years ago, the rank badges were placed on white cloth. The regimental pattern sergeant's arm badge was not worn in the 13th Hussars.

CONTENTS

1: Hussar Regiments 1805 to 1914

3rd The (King's Own) Hussars

Regimental Titles

1685: The Queen Consort's Own Regiment of Dragoons.
1692: The Queen's Dragoons.
1714: The King's Own Regiment of Dragoons.
1751: The 3rd (King's Own) Dragoons.
1818: The 3rd (King's Own) Light Dragoons.
1861: The 3rd (King's Own) Hussars.

Battle Honours to 1914

'Dettingen', 'Salamanca', 'Vittoria', 'Toulouse', 'Peninsula', 'Cabool, 1842', 'Moodkee', 'Ferozeshah', 'Sobraon', 'Chillianwallah', 'Goojerat', 'Punjaub', 'South Africa, 1902'.

4th (Queen's Own) Hussars

Regimental Titles

1685: The Princess Anne of Denmarks Regiment.
1751: 4th Dragoons.
1788: 4th, or Queen's Own Dragoons.
1818: 4th, or (Queen's Own) Light Dragoons.
1861: 4th (Queen's Own) Hussars.

Battle Honours

'Dettingen', 'Talavera', 'Albuhera', 'Salamanca', 'Vittoria', 'Toulouse', 'Peninsula', 'Ghuznee, 1839', 'Afghanistan, 1839', 'Alma', 'Balaclava', 'Inkerman', 'Sevastopol'.

7th Queen's Own Hussars

Regimental Titles

1689: The Queen's Own Dragoons.
1715: The Princess of Wales's Own Royal Dragoons.
1751: 7th or Queen's Own Dragoons.
1784: 7th or Queen's Own Light Dragoons.
1807: 7th (Queen's Own) Light Dragoon Hussars.

1861: 7th The Queen's Own Hussars.
1866: 7th Queen's Own Hussars.

Battle Honours

'Dettingen', 'Warburg', 'Beaumont', 'Willems', 'Orthes', 'Peninsula', 'Waterloo', 'Lucknow', 'South Africa, 1901-02'.

8th (King's Royal Irish) Hussars

Regimental Titles

From the time that the regiment was raised in 1693 until 1751 the regiment was referred to by the Colonel's name, this was accepted practice throughout the army if a regiment did not have a Royal title. From 1751 to 1914 the regiment was styled as follows:

1751: The 8th Dragoons.
1775: The 8th Light Dragoons.
1777: The 8th (King's Royal Irish) Light Dragoons.
1822: 8th The King's Royal Irish (Light) Dragoons (Hussars).
1861: 8th (King's Royal Irish) Hussars.

Battle Honours

'Leswarree', 'Hindoostan', 'Alma', 'Balaclava', 'Inkerman', 'Sevastopol', 'Central India', 'Afghanistan, 1879-80', 'South Africa, 1900-02'.

10th (The Prince of Wales's Own Royal Regiment of Light Dragoons) Hussars

Regimental Titles

From 1715 to 1751 this was a regiment of Dragoons referred to by the Colonel's name.

1751: The 10th Dragoons.
1783: The 10th or Prince of Wales's Own Light Dragoons.
1806: The 10th or Prince of Wales's Own Hussars.
1811: 10th (The Prince of Wales's Own Royal) Light Dragoons (Hussars).
1861: 10th [The Prince of Wales's Own Royal Regiment of Light Dragoons (Hussars)].

Battle Honours

'Warburg', 'Peninsula', 'Waterloo', 'Sevastopol', 'Ali Masjid', 'Afghanistan, 1878-79', 'Egypt, 1884', 'Relief of Kimberley', 'Paardeberg', 'South Africa, 1899-1902'.

The 11th (Prince Albert's Own) Hussars

Regimental Titles

From 1715 to 1751 this was a regiment of Dragoons referred to by the Colonel's name.

1751: The 11th Dragoons.

1783: The 11th Light Dragoons.

1840: The 11th (Prince Albert's Own) Hussars.

Battle Honours

'Egypt and the Sphinx', 'Warburg', 'Beaumont', 'Willems', 'Salamanca', 'Peninsula', 'Waterloo', 'Bhurtpore', 'Alma', 'Balaclava', 'Inkerman', 'Sevastopol'.

13th Hussars

Regimental Titles

From 1715 to 1751 this was a regiment of Dragoons referred to by the Colonel's name.

1751: The 13th Dragoons.

1783: 13th Light Dragoons.

1861: 13th Hussars.

Battle Honours

'Albuhera', 'Vittoria', 'Orthes', 'Toulouse', 'Peninsula', 'Waterloo', 'Alma', 'Balaclava', 'Inkerman', 'Sevastopol', 'Relief of Ladysmith', 'South Africa, 1900-02'.

14th (King's) Hussars

Regimental Titles

From 1715 to 1776 this was referred to by the Colonel's name.

1776: The 14th Light Dragoons.

1798: The 14th (or Duchess of York's Own) Light Dragoons.

1830: The 14th (The King's) Light Dragoons.

1861: 14th (King's) Hussars.

Battle Honours

'Douro', 'Talavera', 'Fuentes d' Onoro', 'Salamanca', 'Vittoria', 'Pyrenees', 'Orthes', 'Peninsula', 'Chillianwallah', 'Goojerat', 'Punjaub', 'Persia', 'Central India', 'Relief of Ladysmith', 'South Africa, 1900-02'.

15th (The King's) Hussars

Regimental Titles

1759:   The 15th Light Dragoons.
1766:   The 15th (or The King's) Light Dragoons.
1807:   The 15th (or The King's) Light Dragoons (Hussars).
1861:   15th (The King's) Hussars.

Battle Honours

'Emsdorf', 'Villiers en Couche', (prior to 1911 this was spelt Villers en Cauchies) 'Willems', 'Egmont-op-Zee', 'Sahagun', 'Vittoria', 'Peninsula', 'Waterloo', 'Afghanistan, 1878-80'.

18th (Queen Mary's Own) Hussars

Regimental Titles

1858:   18th Light Dragoons (Hussars).
1861:   18th Hussars.
1904:   18th Princess of Wales's Hussars.
1905:   18th (Victoria Mary Princess of Wales's Own) Hussars.
1910:   18th (Queen Mary's Own) Hussars.

There was an earlier regiment numbered 18 when the 18th Light Dragoons were converted to Hussars in 1807; this regiment was disbanded in 1821.

Battle Honours

'Peninsula', 'Waterloo', 'Defence of Ladysmith', 'South Africa, 1899-1902'.

The honours for Peninsula and Waterloo were gained by the regiment disbanded in 1821. When the new regiment was raised in 1858 they were authorised to resume the honours of the earlier regiment.

19th (Queen Alexandra's Own Royal) Hussars

Regimental Titles

1858:   The Hon East India Company's 1st Bengal European Regiment.
1861:   The 19th Light Dragoons, changed to The 19th Hussars in the same year.
1885:   The 19th (Princess of Wales's Own) Hussars.

1902:   19th Alexandra Princess of Wales's Own Hussars.
1908:   19th (Queen Alexandra's Own Royal) Hussars.

Battle Honours

'Seringapatam', 'Assaye', 'Niagara', 'Tel-el-Kebir', 'Egypt, 1882-84', 'Abu Klea', 'Nile', 'Defence of Ladysmith', 'South Africa, 1899-1902'.

The honours, Seringapatam, Assaye and Niagara were gained by the 23rd Light Dragoons; this regiment was raised in 1781 and renumbered 19 in 1786. This regiment was converted to Lancers in 1817 and as the 19th Lancers was disbanded in 1821.

20th Hussars

Regimental Titles

1858:   The 2nd Bengal European Light Cavalry.
1861:   The 20th Light Dragoons, the title being changed in the same year to 20th Hussars.

Battle Honours

'Vimiera', 'Peninsula', 'Suakim', 'South Africa, 1901-02'.

The honours for Vimiera and Peninsula were granted to the 20th Light Dragoons, a regiment raised in 1791 and disbanded in 1819.

21st Hussars

Regimental Titles

1858:   3rd Bengal European Light Cavalry.
1861:   21st Light Dragoons, in the same year the title was changed to 21st Hussars.

In 1897 the regiment was converted to Lancers, becoming the 21st Lancers.

2: The Early Period, 1805-1855

WHEN first converted to Hussars all these regiments continued to wear the Light Dragoon jacket. This was the short dark blue garment with silver lace and cords for officers, and white braid lacing for other ranks. The three regiments continued to wear the same facing colour on the collar and cuffs, this being white for the 7th, yellow for the 10th and scarlet for the 15th. The 18th continued to wear their white facings when converted to Hussars in 1807. The jacket and pelisse for all regiments had three rows of buttons, the cord on the officers' dress gradually becoming more elaborate so that by 1807 a definite Hussar uniform had been established.

As Dress Regulations for the Army were not published before 1822 much use has to be made of contemporary illustrations and regimental records to record the first Hussar uniforms and horse furniture. It is fortunate that there are many paintings by well known artists of the period and first amongst these must be Denis Dighton, Junior, whose work is noted for its great attention to detail. He made many paintings of Light Dragoon and Hussar officers during the conversion period. These contemporary illustrations show that the busby was not worn much before 1807 and the first head-dress appears to have been a black cap, cylindrical in shape, with tapering sides and with a peak which could be worn lowered or raised. The shape of this cap was in fact very similar to a mirleton without the wing.

7th HUSSARS: For the 7th the first head-dresses are shown as the black cap, a large black bicorne with a long white over red plume, this hat was worn fore and aft on undress occasions with the very showy mirleton. This head-dress is perhaps of most interest as it was worn for only a very short period. It was also known as a flugelmutze and was copied from those worn by French and German Hussar regiments. Unlike the continental Hussars where this form of head-dress was worn by all ranks, it was only worn by officers in the British regiments. The mirleton for the 7th was light blue with silver lace, the main feature of this head-dress being the long wing which was light blue inside and black outside so that when wound round the cap it appeared black. The first turn of the wing was fixed to the cap with the black outside; on this just above the lower front edge there was a gold and red rosette. A white over red plume was worn on the top of the cap. The heavy cap lines which passed round the cap were gold mixed with crimson and the ends of the lines ended with tassels and flounders. The uniform of the 7th consisted of the jacket and pelisse, white breeches and black hessian boots, while amongst the appointments were the pouch and pouch belt, barrelled sash and sword belt, with slings for the sword and sabretache. The jacket was dark blue with white collar and

ABOVE: Officers of the 7th Hussars 1805 to 1808. The first figure shows the full dress of the regiment in 1807. The second figure shows how the pelisse was usually portrayed in contemporary drawings with only a few of the cords passing across the front to fasten to the buttons. The third and fourth figures show the clothing of 1805 and illustrate the way in which the wing of the mirleton head-dress was allowed to fall either to the front or back of the wearer.

cuffs and silver lace and cords for officers and sergeants. The lace on the collar and cuffs was edged with a line of blue cloth. At first the jackets were of Light Dragoon pattern but by 1807 additional braid had been introduced to make the design more elaborate. The cords and braid on the pelisse were also silver and officers' pelisses were edged with light brown fur. A feature of the officers' pelisse at this time was the five pointed ornament above the cuff. The pouch belt for officers of the 7th was gold laced edged with red, and the pouch itself appears to have been faced with white cloth edged with gold, and bore the Queen's Cypher and crown as shown on the sabretache and shabraque (see Fig 1).

The barrel sash worn round the waist was crimson and gold and was worn by officers of all Hussar regiments up to 1855. The sash was made up of lengths of crimson cord and eighteen gilt barrels; the cord was doubled and passed round the waist three times, the barrels then being placed to form three rows of six, although illustrations show that at

11

times the barrels were placed in an irregular manner. The ends of the cords were looped at the back and passed round the right hip to be looped through the front part of the sash. The ends then passed over to hang in front, the ends being finished with gold bullion tassels. The officer's sword belt and the slings for the sword and sabretache were

gold laced edged with red. The sabretache was made of red leather with a pocket at the back, the front being faced with white cloth and edged with gold lace, with the red leather forming a narrow outer edge to the lace. The embroidered design on the face was a crown over the doubled and reversed cypher 'C.R.' This was Queen Charlotte's cypher. The officers' boots were black hessians with black tassels and gilt spurs.

Officers are mostly shown with a Mameluke hilt pattern curved sword in a scabbard that was black with gilt mountings. This type of sword was of a pattern popular with Light Dragoon and Hussar officers and eventually became a Levée Dress sword for the officers of some Hussar regiments. The regulation sword at this period was the 1796 Light Cavalry pattern.

For other ranks the uniform followed the same pattern of the officers but with a much more simplified system of white braiding on the jacket and pelisse. On the jacket the white collar was edged top and bottom with a line of blue cloth inside the corded edges. The cuffs also had a line of blue cloth showing between the top of the cuff and the braided ornamental knot. The pelisse for other ranks was edged with white fur. The pouch belt was white as also was the sword belt and the slings for the sword and sabretache. The sword was the curved bladed 1796 Light Cavalry Pattern with stirrup hilt. The scabbard was steel and the sabretache for other ranks was of plain black leather. The boots for other ranks were shaped similar to those of the officers, being black hessians with black tassels and steel spurs.

10th HUSSARS: On conversion to Hussars the 10th retained the yellow facings they had worn as Light Dragoons until 1811 when on becoming a Royal regiment the facings were changed to scarlet. The details of the first Hussar clothing for the regiment follow the pattern of the 7th except for the regimental distinctions. The head-dresses were the black cap, bicorne and mirleton. The mirleton for the 10th was scarlet and black edged with gold lace and with a pattern of circles made up of gold lace running through the centre of the scarlet inside of the wing. The outside of the wing was black and the first fold round the cap had a gold and red rosette in the centre. A white over red plume was worn on top of the cap. The gold cap lines were looped round the body of the cap and fastened on the right side. The ends falling in front ended with gold tassels and flounders. A Dighton painting dated 1805 shows this head-dress and another painting shows an officer of the same date wearing a similar mirleton but edged with silver lace and with a

ABOVE: Officers of the 10th Hussars 1805 to 1808. The first, second and fourth figures are dated 1805 and the third figure 1808. The uniforms are described in the text but the figures illustrate the way in which the clothing and appointments were worn. The main items of interest are the mirleton head-dress, the two patterns of swords, the black ties to the second figure's pelisse and the yellow boots of the fourth figure.

silver lace worm running through the centre of the wing. The cap lines and plume were the same as for gold laced mirleton. The jacket was dark blue with yellow collar and cuffs and was laced and corded in silver, the pelisse also being dark blue and laced in the same manner as the jacket. The pelisse is shown to have black fur in 1805 but by 1806 it is shown as grey. Grey fur was also shown again in 1808 and 1809. The lining of the pelisse was crimson; the officer of 1805 has black cord ties to his pelisse but all other illustrations show silver. The pouch belt was silver laced and had a yellow edging but the sword belt, sword and sabretache slings were of crimson leather embroidered with silver. The officer's sabretache was made of crimson leather and the front was faced with scarlet cloth and bore the device of the Prince of Wales's feathers and motto, below which was a crown above the doubled and reversed cypher 'G.R.' The lace round the edge of the front was silver. Most of the paintings show the officers carrying the regulation stirrup hilted sword in a steel scabbard but one portrait of 1805 shows that the sword with the Mameluke hilt was carried in the regiment.

The gold and crimson barrel sash was worn, also white breeches,

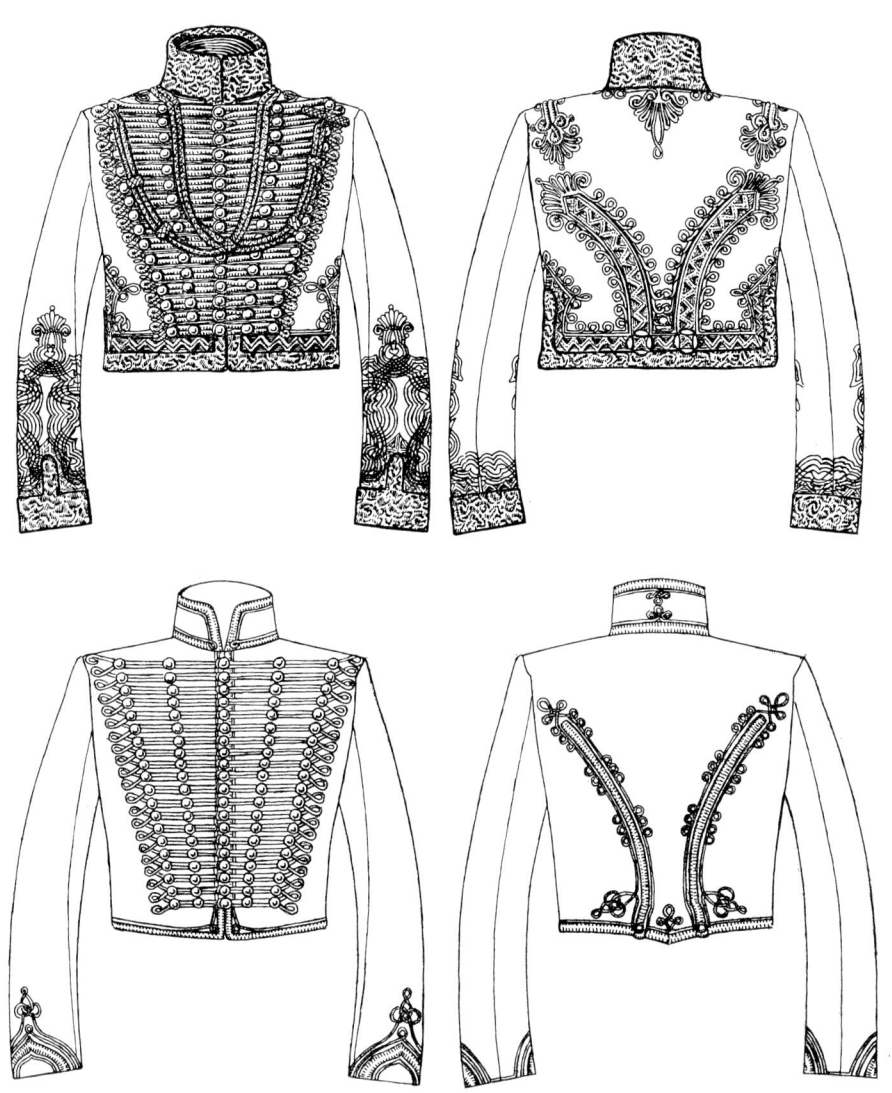

*TOP: 15th Hussars. This pattern of pelisse was worn by officers until
1830 when the Regulations ordered Hussar regiments to change the
colour from blue to scarlet and at the same time the silver lace of the
15th was changed to gold. The pelisse illustrated was probably introduced
in the regiment between 1820 and 1822 and was made of dark blue cloth
edged all round the collar, cuffs and body of the garment with black
astrakhan, the buttons, lace and braid being silver. The very complicated
design on the cuffs was made up of five rows of tracing braid.*

*BOTTOM: A private's jacket, 7th Hussars, 1815. A jacket of this type was
originally in the Cotton Museum. Troop Sergeant Major Cotton who had
served in the 7th Hussars was the guide to the Field of Waterloo and
he opened a museum which displayed relics of the battle. This jacket
was amongst the items displayed. It had originally belonged to a Private
Simmonds of the regiment and was left to the Cotton Museum when he
died.*

black hessian boots with gold rims and tassels and gilt spurs. A feature of the 10th Hussars' dress at this period was that the braid above the cuff was shaped in three loops probably to represent the feathers of the Prince of Wales's crest, the Prince of Wales being the Colonel of the regiment. In the painting dated 1805, showing the mirleton with gold lace, the officer is also shown wearing yellow hessian boots; there are very few references to this type of footwear and it may be that for a few years the regiment copied the continental style of footwear as most of the European armies could show Cavalry officers wearing either scarlet, crimson, green or yellow boots. For other ranks of the 10th Hussars the dress of the men followed the same pattern as the officers but in a much simpler form. The head-dress was the light brown fur busby with a short white over red plume and white cord cap lines while the busby bag was unusual in being yellow. The jacket was dark blue with yellow collar and cuffs and was laced with silver for sergeants and white for other ranks. The pelisse was also dark blue with lacing similar to the jacket but was unusual in that the braiding was edged with a frame of silver or white braid. The fur edging to the other ranks' pelisse was white. White breeches and black hessian boots with black tassels and white metal spurs were worn. The sword belt and slings were white, the sabretache being black with white slings. The sword was of the 1796, Light Cavalry Pattern with stirrup hilt and steel scabbard.

Paintings that show other ranks of the 7th and 10th dated 1808 show the barrel sash worn round the waist to be made up of black cords and white metal barrels although it is probable that they were dark blue and white. For both these regiments the officers are shown wearing a black neckerchief round the neck, this being tied in front with the ends flared out. Above this the ends of the white collar showed and at the base of the jacket collar a white shirt frill jutted out. For other ranks a black stock was worn round the neck but with no protruding ends and a white shirt frill appeared from inside the front collar opening.

15th HUSSARS: Contemporary illustrations showing officers of the 15th before they received the fur head-dress in July 1807 only show the bicorne hat being worn, but records of the period from 1805 to 1807 show that the regiment was fully clothed and equipped as Hussars with the arrival of the fur busbies. The uniform for officers is shown in the paintings of Robert Dighton, dated 1808. Unlike the other regiments the fur cap was made of black fur with a red bag and a white over red plume and gold cap lines ending in tassels and flounders. The jacket was dark blue with scarlet collar and cuffs but the silver cords on the front were not as elaborate as for the 7th and 10th regiments, the pattern of lacing was similar but the narrow braiding each side of the outer buttons did not extend between the rows of cord. Above the cuff an ornamental figure similar to an Austrian knot was worn, this figuring being traced all round and below with a thin tracing braid. The pouch belt is shown as being gold, laced with an edging of red. This gold and red was shown between 1805 and 1808 until in August 1808 the officers received new silver laced belts. The pelisse was dark blue like the jacket and was laced with silver in the same way, the fur edging for the pelisse was black. A gold and crimson sash was worn

ABOVE: 15th Hussars, Officer in Review Order, 1813.

ABOVE: The first and second figures represent officers of the 15th Hussars at 1805 and 1808. The third figure is based on a contemporary print and represents the 7th Hussars in 1812. The uniform was dark blue with gold lace and braid with blue pantaloons embroidered in gold. The fourth figure, based on the same series of prints, shows an officer of the 18th Hussars in 1812. The busby bag and pelisse lining are light blue. The jacket is dark blue with white collar and cuffs. White breeches are worn, and the back of the sabretache is crimson.

round the waist. White breeches were worn and black hessian boots, the top rim of the boots being edged with silver braid and with silver tassels in front. The sword belt was made of crimson leather ornamented with silver embroidery as were the sword and sabretache slings. The scarlet faced sabretache was edged with silver lace and the design on the face was embroidered in gold showing the doubled and reversed cypher 'G.R.' with a crown above. Above the crown was a scroll with the words 'The King's'. Officers are shown with either the stirrup hilt or Mameluke hilted sword. For officers of the 7th, 10th and 15th the clasps on the sword belts and the buckles on the sword and sabretache slings appear to be of the lion's head type.

For other ranks the dress was less elaborate than that for the officers. The fur head-dress was light brown with a red busby bag, a short stubby white over red plume, and white cap lines. The jacket had a red collar and cuffs and white braid, the pelisse was edged with black fur, and the rest of the uniform comprised white breeches and belts, black hessian boots with black tassels and a black sabretache. A sergeant

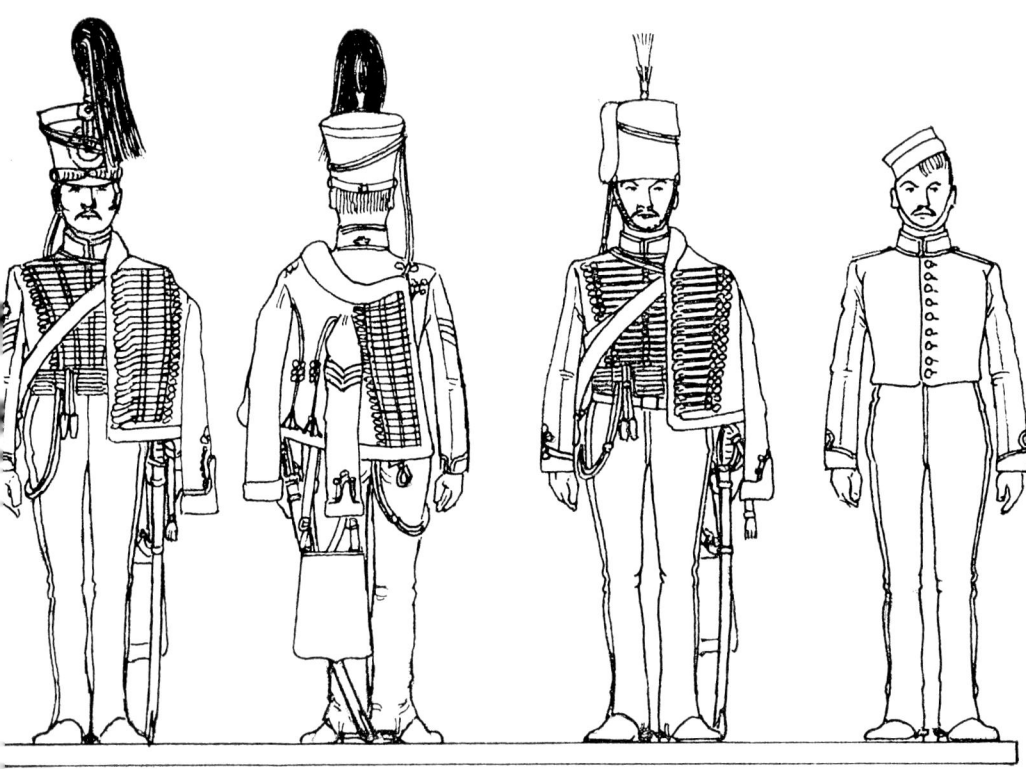

ABOVE: The uniform for other ranks in 1832. For sergeants the lace was gold and for ranks below, the lace was yellow worsted. The badges of rank were worn on the right sleeve of the jacket and pelisse. The second figure showing the rear view is wearing the white overalls that were worn in drill order. The third figure shows the last pattern of full dress worn by other ranks before the introduction of the tunic. The fourth figure shows a private in stable dress. The jacket was dark blue with yellow piping on the collar and cuffs.

is shown as having light brown fur on his pelisse and on the right arm of his jacket above the elbow are three gold chevrons on red cloth. Above the chevrons is a gold crown; this appears to have been a distinction of the 15th Hussars at this period. Although chevrons were issued for general wear by NCOs in 1802 they had already been worn in some regiments previous to this date. The 1802 regulation quotes three bars for a sergeant. The sergeant's barrel sash is shown as being crimson and gold as worn by officers, the sword carried is the stirrup hilt Light Cavalry Pattern.

18th HUSSARS: The earliest pictures that show the dress for officers are dated 1808. The two figures that show the uniform are standing half turned to the right. The head-dress is the brown fur busby, with a bright blue bag, a white over red plume and gold cap lines. The jacket is dark blue with white collar and cuffs and silver cords on the front; a gold and crimson barrel sash is worn but the pouch belt is not shown. White breeches and black hessian boots with black tassels and gilt spurs complete the dress. Both officers are carrying the sword slung

KEY TO FIGURES: 1: 7th Hussars, Officer, 1805. 2: 15th Hussars, Officer, 1809. 3: 18th Hussars, Officer, 1814. 4: 10th Hussars, Trooper, 1813. 5: 15th Hussars, Trooper, 1811. 6: 15th Hussars, Trooper, 1813. 7: 15th Hussars, Officer, 1813. 8: 10th Hussars, Officer, 1825. 9: 15th Hussars, Officer, 1825. 10: 8th Hussars, Officer, 1830. 11: 7th Hussars, Officer, 1833. 12: 8th Hussars, Trooper, 1833.

KEY TO FIGURES: 13: 10th Hussars, Trooper, 1834. 14: 15th Hussars, Trooper, 1833. 15: 8th Hussars, Officer, 1850. 16: 11th Hussars, Officer, 1848. 17: 11th Hussars, Officer, 1854. 18: 8th Hussars, Trooper, 1854. 19: 18th Hussars, Officer, 1858. 20: 11th Hussars, Officer, 1865. 21: 19th Hussars, Sergeant, 1895. 22: 8th Hussars, Trooper, 1895. 23: 11th Hussars, Trooper, 1895. 24: 4th Hussars, Trooper, 1895.

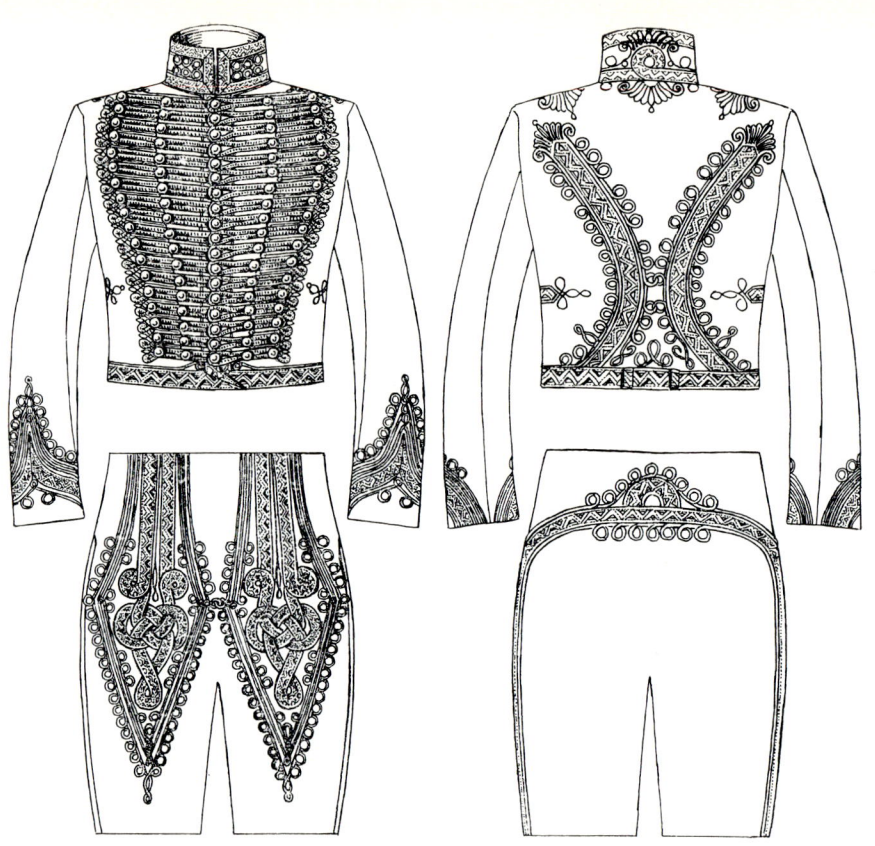

The Full Dress jacket and pantaloons worn in Levée Dress by officers of the 15th Hussars, c. 1817-1822. Both garments are dark blue with silver lace and braid, the five rows of buttons on the jacket are silver. The Levée Dress pantaloons were only worn on special occasions such as Court functions or Balls and were never worn on mounted or dismounted regimental parades. All Hussar regiments had pantaloons of this type but with lace and braid placed on according to regimental design, this type of garment was worn until the introduction of the tunic. According to Dress Regulations 1822 the 7th Hussars were permitted to continue wearing blue pantaloons while the colour given for the other regiments was scarlet.

over the arm so that the hilt does not show but the first picture shows a steel scabbard and the second a black gilt mounted one so that it is probable that both the stirrup hilt and Mameluke patterns were used in the regiment. The colours of the sabretache are not shown but officers of a later date have a pattern faced with bright blue cloth edged with silver lace. No picture of any other rank is shown but their dress almost certainly followed the pattern of the three regiments already in existence.

Once the Hussar uniform had become established it was not long before certain articles were found to be unsuitable. The white breeches were not convenient for every day wear and the tall full busby proved to be very cumbersome and almost unmanageable when the men were mounted. This head-dress was gradually replaced by a form of shako for ordinary parades and with service dress. The fur busby was retained only for dress parades.

For the 7th an officer of 1808 is shown wearing a brown shako. This is most likely to be of the type referred to as a castor cap, which was a form of shako covered with beaver fur which clipped very close and having the appearance of being made of brown velvet. A regulation of 1812 gives the 7th Hussars a blue shako while a contemporary painting shows other ranks of the 10th wearing a black peakless shako, this being replaced in 1813 by a scarlet shako. The 15th also received their scarlet pattern in the same year.

The Regulation for the Clothing of the Cavalry, 1812, gives the 7th as now to have jackets with blue collar and cuffs made of the same materials as the jacket. For officers the jacket and pelisse was to be trimmed with gold lace and braid in place of silver, while for the men's jackets and pelisses the white braid was to be replaced by yellow. Blue overalls were now worn and the campaign overalls were grey with a double white stripe down the sides. It seems that with this change of uniform the number of buttons on the jacket and pelisse were increased to five rows. Two jackets worn by troopers of the 7th Hussars at Waterloo were known to be in museums some years ago and both garments had twenty rows of cord across the front and five rows of buttons. With the jacket mention is made of a pair of dark blue overalls having a single yellow stripe and a yellow and red barrelled sash.

By 1819, according to Marcuard's chart showing the uniforms of the British Army, the 7th Hussars now had a gold laced light blue shako, this with an upright white over red feather. The 10th had black drooping feathers on a gold laced black shako while the 15th are shown with a gold laced scarlet shako. The 18th are shown as still wearing the fur cap with a blue bag. In 1821 the 18th Hussars were disbanded and with this disbandment the Hussar busby disappeared for a number of years.

With the conversion of the 8th Light Dragoons to Hussars in 1822 this now made up the number of Hussar regiments to four numbered the 7th, 8th, 10th and 15th and all wearing the shako. A full description of this head-dress as applied to the 7th and 10th regiments is given in the *Dress Regulations of 1822: 'Shako*—black beaver, bell shaped, $8\frac{1}{2}$ inches deep with glazed black top about $10\frac{1}{2}$ inches in diameter, a two inch band round the top formed of narrow gold French braid circles, a narrow French braid round the bottom, a gold Russian braid wheel in the centre, communicating by a chain loop to a large Royal cord rosette at the top. Gilt chin scales and rose fastenings. A gold cord encircling the shako three times, suspended on either side by a gilt lion's-head ring, being tied in a knot on the right side and having a loop to fasten it occasionally to the buttons of the jacket. Black patent leather peak in front and another always turned up at the back of the shako, both edged with French braid. Black drooping cockstail feathers.'

Although a silver laced regiment the 15th had a scarlet shako with gold lace and cap lines and the 8th had a black silver laced shako with gold cap lines, Details of individual items of uniform and equipment

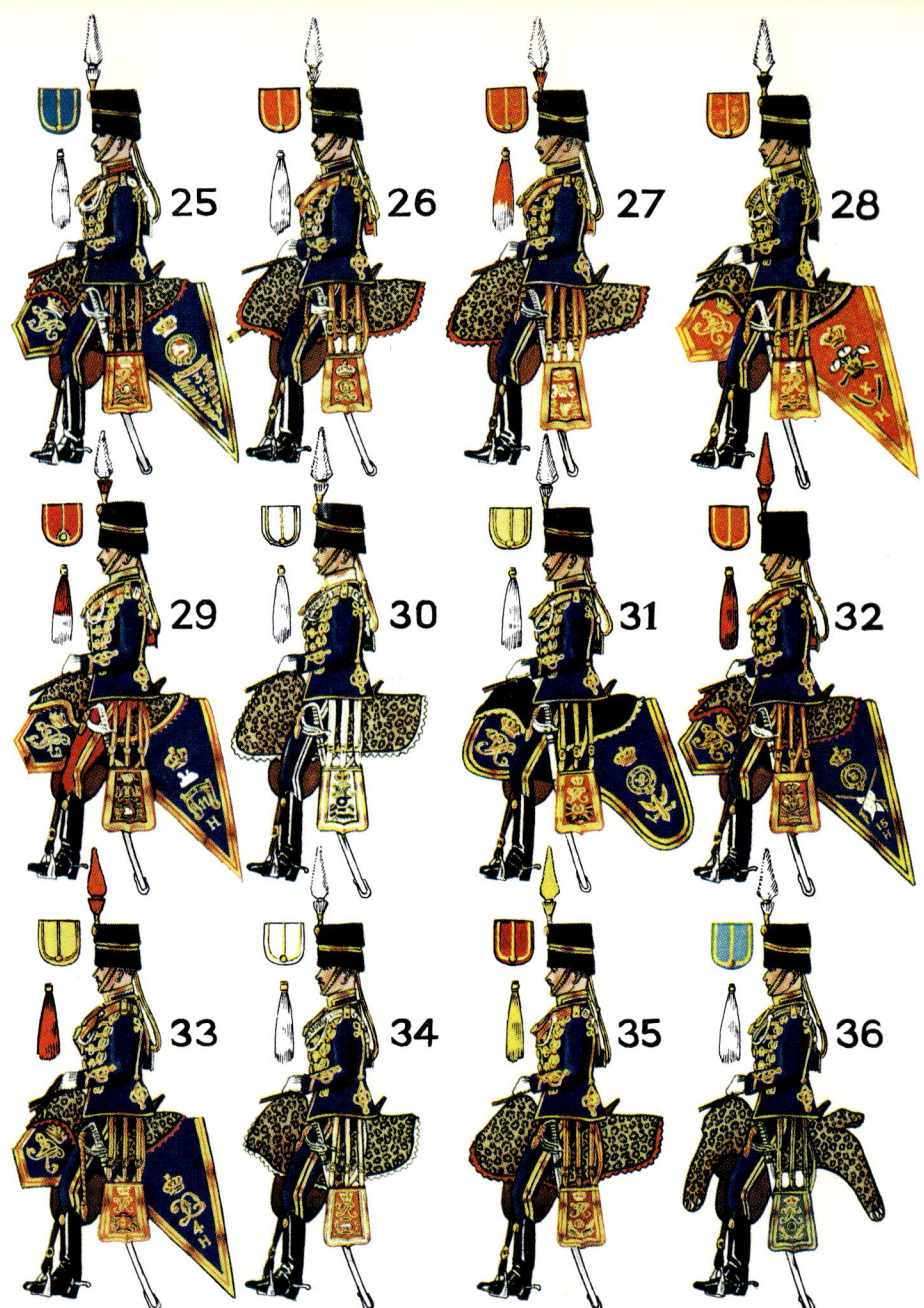

Officers in Review Order and Full Dress prior to the abolition of the sabretache and shabraque. KEY TO FIGURES: 25: 3rd The (King's Own) Hussars. 26: 7th Queen's Own Hussars. 27: 8th (King's Royal Irish) Hussars. 28: 10th (The Prince of Wales's Own Royal) Hussars. 29: 11th (Prince Albert's Own) Hussars. 30: 13th Hussars. 31: 14th (King's) Hussars. 32: 15th (The King's) Hussars. 33: 4th (Queen's Own) Hussars. 34: 19th (Queen Alexandra's Own Royal) Hussars. 35: 20th Hussars. 36: 21st Hussars.

KEY TO FIGURES: 37: 11th Hussars, Reg't'l. Quartermaster Sergeant, 1897. 38: 13th Hussars, Regimental Sergeant-Major, 1897. 39: 3rd Hussars, Trooper—Drill order, 1897. 40: 13th Hussars, Trooper—Marching order, 1897. 41: 15th Hussars Officer—Review order, 1905. 42: 3rd Hussars, Officer—Drill order, 1905. 43: 14th Hussars, Officer—Serge frock, 1900. 44: 7th Hussars, Officer, 1903. 45: 11th Hussars, Officer, 1911. 46: 4th Hussars, Trooper, 1911. 47: 8th Hussars, Sergeant, 1911. 48: 18th Hussars, Corporal, 1911.

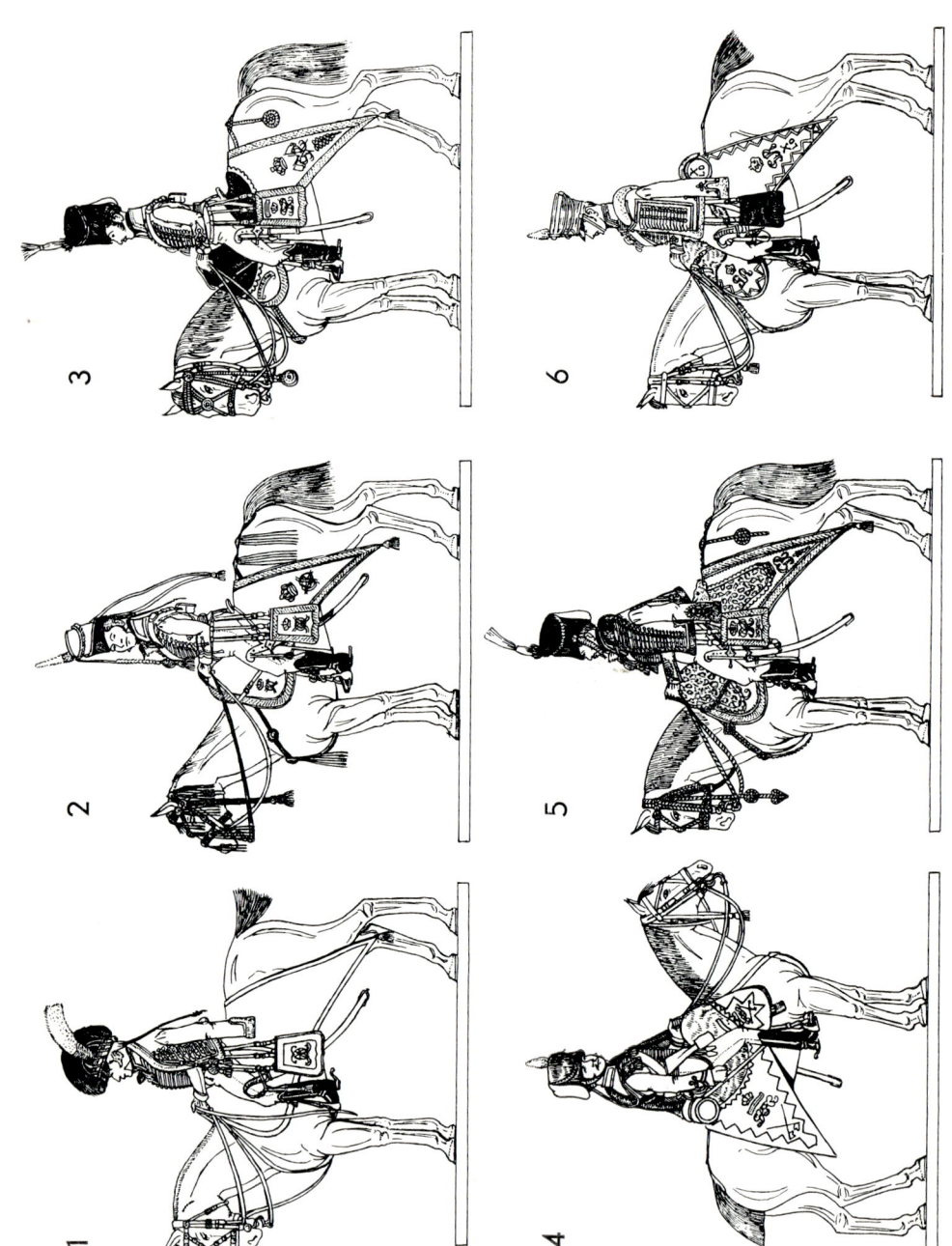

noted before the first issue of *Dress Regulations* in 1822 include a new pattern lace on the officers' jackets and pelisses. This was of the type known as 'chain gimp' and was worn on officer' tunics until 1914. This lace replaced the cord in 1817. In the same year the Staff officers of the 15th were ordered to wear cocked hats and the red collar and cuffs of the regiment were changed to blue of the same material as the jacket. With the 1822 Regulations there were still five rows of buttons on the jacket and pelisse, with silver lace for the 15th and 8th and gold for the 7th and 10th. For Full Dress and Levée Dress, scarlet overalls and pantaloons are quoted although the 7th kept to blue while for occasions other than Full Dress, overalls of a blueish grey colour were worn. These overalls were cut very wide at the knee and tapered in to the ankles and were referred to as cossacks.

In 1830 the 8th and 15th were ordered to change the silver lace on their uniforms to gold so that now all regiments had gold lace for officers and yellow for other ranks.

The most noticeable change in clothing took place when a General Order of August 2, 1830, directed that the colour of the pelisse should be changed from blue to scarlet. This was shortly after the accession of

---

OPPOSITE PAGE:

1: This illustration of an officer of a Light Dragoon regiment in 1801 shows that even before the conversion to Hussars the pelisse and sabretache had been introduced into the Light Dragoons. These items were copied from the Continental Hussar regiments. The officer shown belongs to the 7th Light Dragoons.

2: 7th Light Dragoons. Officer 1805. This officer shows the real beginnings of the Hussar clothing and appointments in the British army. The whole appearance was much more after the Continental fashion especially the mirleton head-dress and the decoration of the harness. For the colours of the uniform and shabraque see Figure 1. The decoration on the black leather horse trappings is made of black cord, this style of decoration being copied from the Polish cavalry.

3: The 15th Hussars, 1809. This officer in Full Dress does not wear his pelisse. This garment was usually worn during the winter months. In the summer it was worn only in Review Order or when ordered. Although very decorative the pelisse was in fact worn as an overcoat for protection from the weather. In this drawing the bridle and leatherwork ornamented with shells can be seen.

4: A trooper of Hussars, 1811. The regiment shown is the 15th—see Figure 5. By this time the clothing and appointments of Hussars had become well established. The weapons for other ranks were the sword and carbine. In this illustration the carbine is passed through a slit in the sheepskin and shabraque and fitted into a small leather bucket. Illustrations of the period show the carbine also suspended from the swivel of the carbine belt.

5: The 18th Hussars, 1814—see Figure 3. The splendours of the saddlery and bridles used by officers of European Hussar regiments can be seen in this illustration of an officer of 18th Hussars. The black leather covered with cowrie shells was a fashion copied from the Zeiten Hussars of the Prussian army.

6: A trooper of the 10th Hussars, 1815. Figure 4 shows the colours of this uniform except that the head-dress shown here is the red shako with a white band beneath the top edge and a short stubby white over red plume. This shako was issued to the regiment in 1813. Unlike the sabretaches of the officers, that of other ranks was plain black with only two slings. The leather for the bridle and reins was brown.

ABOVE:

15th (The King's Hussars. The last pattern sabretache worn by officers of the regiment until 1902.

OPPOSITE PAGE:

The indication of rank worn on the collar and cuffs from 1855 to 1902. KEY: Fig 1, sleeve detail for Colonel, Lieutenant-Colonel and Major. Fig 2, collar detail for Colonel, Lieutenant-Colonel and Major, all regiments except the 3rd and 13th Hussars. Fig 3, collar detail for Colonel, Lieutenant-Colonel and Major 3rd Hussars. Fig 4, collar detail for Colonel, Lieutenant-Colonel and Major, 13th Hussars. Fig 5, sleeve detail for Captains, all regiments. Fig 6, collar details for Captains, all regiments except 3rd and 13th Hussars. Fig 7, sleeve ornaments for Lieutenants and 2nd Lieutenants, all regiments. Fig 8, collar detail for Lieutenants and 2nd Lieutenants, 3rd Hussars. Fig 9, collar detail for Lieutenants and 2nd Lieutenants, all regiments except 3rd and 13th Hussars. From 1902 until 1914 the sleeve ornament for all ranks of officers was the same as Fig 7, the collars being laced as Fig 9.

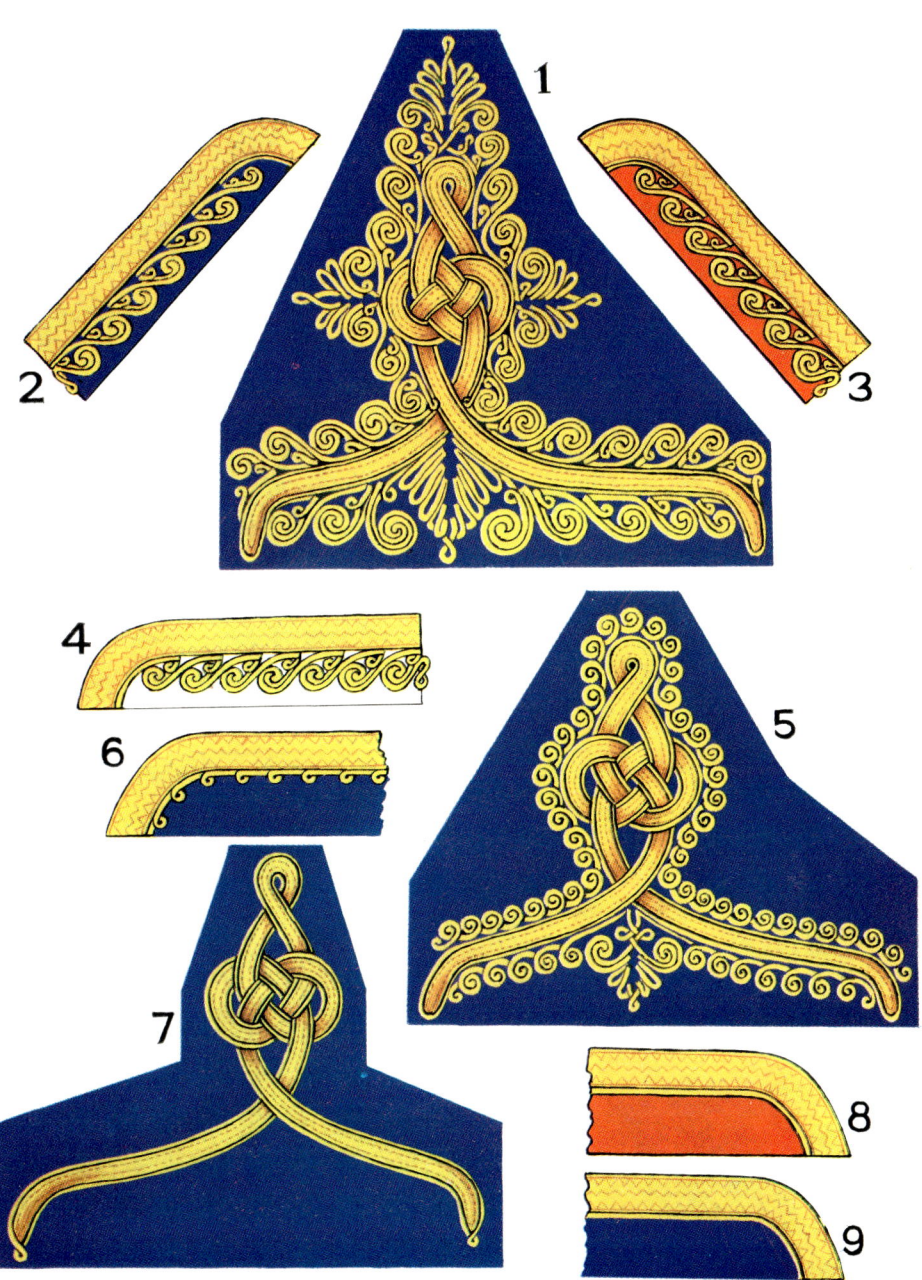

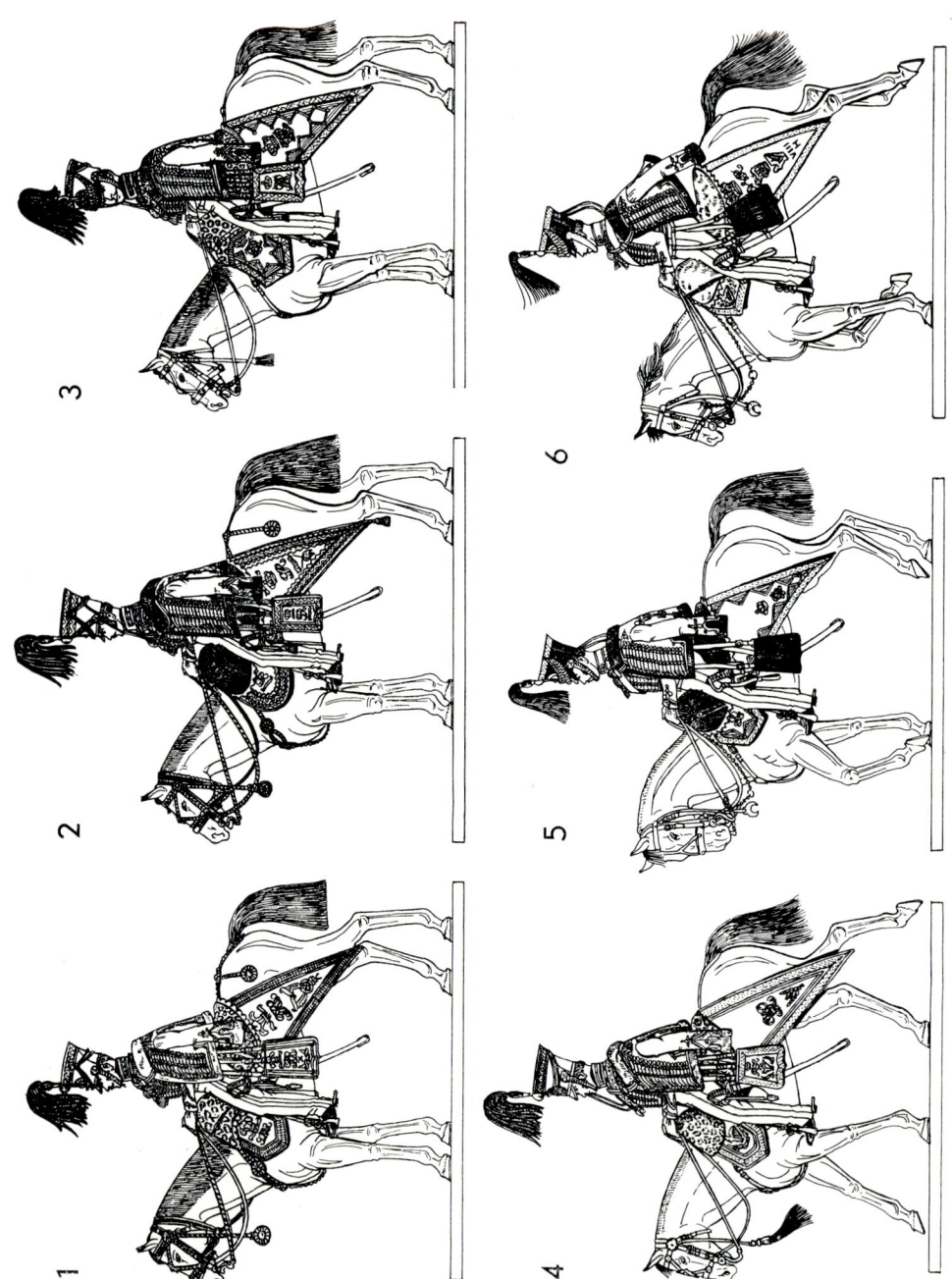

King William IV in 1830 when the King directed that all Cavalry regiments with the exception of the Royal Horse Guards should be dressed in scarlet. The scarlet pelisses were replaced again by blue by 1844. A Submission dated March 14, 1840, gives the date for this change to be completed by March 31, 1844.

During this period the white sheepskins were replaced by black in 1834.

For the 7th, the other ranks' uniform was now a black shako, slightly taller than regulation size. This appears to have been distinctive to the 7th. Round the top of the shako was a band of yellow lace. On the front centre of this band was a yellow card boss. On the front of the shako was a circle of yellow lace which had a central stripe of red. This circle of lace had a button placed in the centre and the lace was connected to the boss by two loops of yellow lace. The plume was made up of black horsehair and across the front of the head-dress was a festoon of yellow cords ending with cap lines which were connected to the front of

---

OPPOSITE PAGE:
1: The 10th Hussars, Officer, 1825. The cowrie shells that decorated the leatherwork of the officers' horses was continued throughout the life of the 10th although after 1914 the occasions on which it could be seen were very few. Early prints and pictures of the regiment do not show the pattern of the shells very clearly but at some time shortly after becoming Hussars the shells were placed in groups of three resembling the Prince of Wales's Plumes. For the colour of the uniform and shabraque see Figure 8.

2: The 15th Hussars, 1825. A feature of the 15th Hussars was the scarlet shako, rather taller than quoted in the regulations. It was decorated with gold lace and cap lines in spite of the fact that the 15th were a silver laced regiment. Figure 9 shows the colours for the officers' dress and appointments, this being the last dress before the order changing the lace to gold. For Hussar regiments except the 10th the practice of ornamenting the leatherwork with shells began to fade out at this period to be replaced by a more regulation pattern.

3: Officer, 7th Hussars, 1833. The uniforms for officers of Hussar regiments had now reached their most elaborate form. All regiments had gold lace intersected by a narrow gold tracing cord which had the effect of heightening the brilliance of the gold lace. Figure 11 illustrates this uniform and also shows the very handsome shabraque used by the 7th Hussars.

4: 8th Hussars, officer, 1830. This officer is wearing the last silver laced uniform worn by officers of the regiment. Figure 10 which illustrates this uniform has an almost Hanoverian appearance. Features of the 8th Hussars at this period were the gold cap lines ending in acorns and the horse's face piece decorated with a silver star. The leather was brown.

5: Trooper, 7th Hussars, 1834. The dress for other ranks at this time was very similar in style but less elaborate than that worn by the officers, all the lace and braid being yellow while the belts and sword and sabretache slings were white. The sabretache was plain black with two slings. The shabraque was of a pattern like the officers' but with yellow lace and braid. The leather was brown and the horse's face piece was of the inverted 'Y' type. Of interest is the crescent throat ornament. This type of ornament had been used by Continental cavalry for many years. It can be seen in most of the illustrations of Napoleon's cavalry regiments.

6: 8th Hussars, trooper, 1833. Almost identical to the 7th the real identification between the regiments was the difference in the shabraque. This is shown in Figure 12. In 1833 the sheepskin covering the saddle was white. As in the 7th, the clothing for other ranks was a less elaborate form of the officer's dress with yellow cords and braids.

ABOVE: 10th Hussars, Officer in Review Order, 1833.

the jacket. A yellow metal chin chain was worn.

The jacket was dark blue with yellow cords and five rows of buttons while the scarlet pelisse with yellow cords and five rows of buttons was trimmed round the edges with black Astrakhan. The blue overalls had a single yellow stripe. A white pouch belt was worn, and the waist belt with sword and sabretache slings was also white. With this uniform a crimson and yellow sash was worn round the waist. This was the Hussar pattern made with crimson cords and yellow metal barrels. The sabretache was black suspended from two slings, the sword still being the old pattern, as the 1822 pattern had not yet been issued to the regiment. The other ranks' shabraque was of a very attractive pattern which was similar to the type used by the Prussian Hussar regiments, of the same shape as the officers (Fig 11), but the lace was yellow. The shabraque was dark blue edged with yellow lace. Inside the lace was a border of scarlet vandykes which were edged with yellow cord, the only embroidery was the crown over 'Q.O.,' cypher on front and rear corners. The sheepskin which was white until 1834 was altered to black. The reins, bridle and all leather accoutrements were brown.

The other ranks' dress for the 8th Hussars was almost identical to that of the 7th. As with the other regiments during this period the only real means of identification was on mounted duties when the regimental pattern shabraque was used. The 8th Hussars' dress was the regulation shako coloured exactly as described for the 7th. With regard to the jacket, scarlet pelisse, and blue overalls, a broad yellow stripe, the crimson and yellow barrel sash, and white belts and slings. The regiment had been issued with the 1822 pattern sword. This had a three bar hilt and the blade was slightly curved. The sabretache was black (Fig 12). The shabraque was made of dark blue cloth and was edged all round with a border of yellow lace. On the front part the design was a harp with a wreath of shamrock all embroidered yellow. On the rear part, the design consisted of a crown above the 'W.R.,' cypher, and below this there was a Lion on Crown, Harp and 'VIII H.' all yellow. As in the other regiments the sheepskin was changed to black in 1834. For the 10th the other ranks' dress was as for the 8th except that the 1822 pattern sword was not issued to the regiment until 1834. Like the other regiments the shabraque for the 10th was very elaborate (Fig 13), being made of scarlet cloth with a yellow lace border. This lace had two narrow blue stripes. Unlike the other regiments there was no design on the front part but on the rear corners was a finely embroidered design of the Prince of Wales's Feathers in white, with the motto scrolls blue, edged yellow, and bearing the words 'ICH DIEN' in yellow. The crown on the lower part of the feathers was yellow; below this in white was the doubled and reversed cypher 'W.R.' Beneath this were two scrolls edged yellow with the honours 'Peninsula' and 'Waterloo' in yellow on a blue ground. Below this was the numeral 'X' enclosed in a blue horseshoe shaped scroll, this scroll bearing the title 'Prince of Wales's Own'. Around the scrolls were sprays of laurel embroidered in white. The other ranks of the 15th Hussars followed the other regiments as far as dress was concerned with the exception of the shako. This was the scarlet head-dress peculiar to the 15th. The body of the shako was scarlet laced in the same way as the black shakos, but a contemporary painting shows

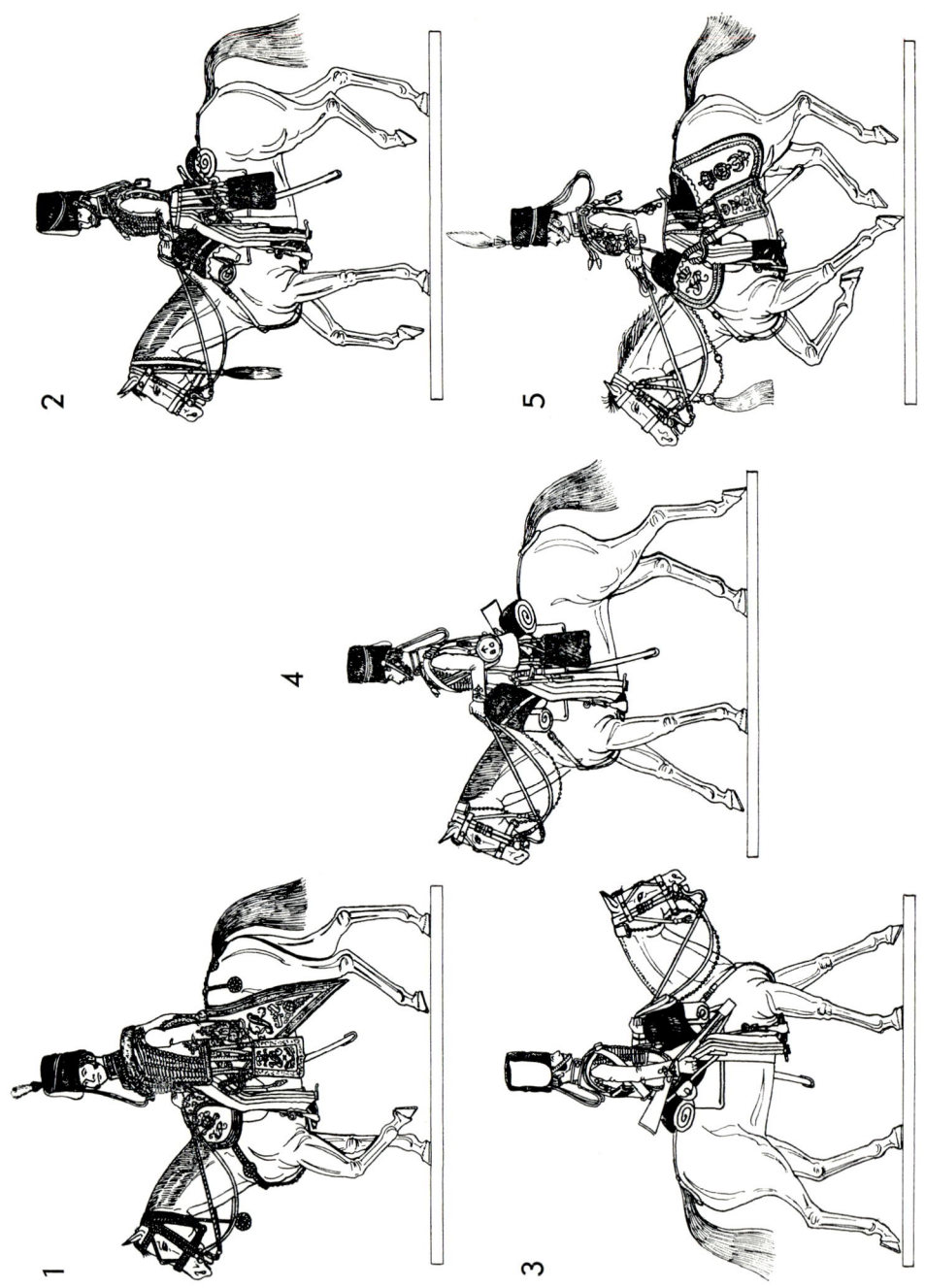

that the cords encircling the head-dress were not festooned across the front (Fig 14). The shako for the 15th, like that of the 7th was slightly taller than the regulation pattern. The shabraque was of blue cloth with a border of yellow lace. The design on the rear corners consisted of a crown over the doubled and reversed cypher 'W.R.' all in yellow embroidery. Below this on a red scroll the honour 'Emsdorf' above crossed white flags, below the flags 'XV' and 'K.H.' in yellow. On the front part partly hidden by the sheepskin was a crown above the royal cypher and a red scroll bearing the honour 'EMSDORF'.

While for this period the dress for other ranks has been described the dress for officers was of the same general pattern but in a much more elaborate form as can be seen by the 7th Hussar officer (Fig 11). The head-dress had large plumes of black cocks' feathers. These feathers are often shown in paintings as being of a green colour but although on this type of feather a greenish sheen would appear the general effect would be black. A really striking feature of this dress was the sabretache which while plain black for other ranks had, since conversion from Light Dragoons, become very ornate for the officers and could now be described as a form of regimental badge. The shabraque also was now at its most elaborate and the officers' pattern was as described for other ranks but

OPPOSITE PAGE:

1: This officer of the 10th Hussars, 1845 is shown wearing the fur head-dress shortly after it was restored to the regiment. The illustration shows the Full Dress worn until the Crimean War. The distinctive badge of the regiment, the Prince of Wales's Plumes and Motto can be seen on the fore part and rear portion of the shabraque and on the sabretache. The sword carried by officers of the 10th Hussars was of the 1822 Light Cavalry officer's pattern.

2: An officer of the 11th Hussars, 1854. This was the dress worn at Balaclava. The busby without the plume, the full dress jacket, pouch and pouch belt, with the full dress sword belt and slings and a plain black leather sabretache. Booted overalls strapped below the boot were worn. Figure 17 gives the colour for this uniform. The horse's throat plume was crimson over white.

3: A trooper of the 11th Hussars, 1854. This was one of the regiments that formed the Light Brigade at Balaclava and led by Lord Cardigan took part in the famous charge. This offside view shows the method by which the carbine was held in place. The trooper's uniform worn during the charge was the fur busby without plume, the dress jacket and crimson overalls and the barrelled sash.

4: The nearside view of a trooper of the 8th Hussars 1854. Figure 18 shows the details of this trooper's uniform and horse furniture. The 8th were another of the regiments forming part of the Light Brigade at Balaclava and the illustrations show how the regiment appeared during the charge. The blue water canteen which was marked with the Board of Ordnance sign had a brown leather strap and the white haversack with a white strap were carried at the left hip. The illustrations showing Hussars in 1854 represent the end of the period when the jacket and pelisse were worn.

5: The 14th Hussars, officer, 1861. The change from Light Dragoons did not make a very great change in the appearance of the 14th, the most important change being that the small Light Dragoon shako was replaced by a fur busby and the tunic had six rows of gold lace instead of the five rows worn as Light Dragoons. Booted overalls were still worn and the Light Dragoon pattern pouch belt and pouch was still retained as also was the shabraque which for the 14th was dark blue with gold lace and embroidery.

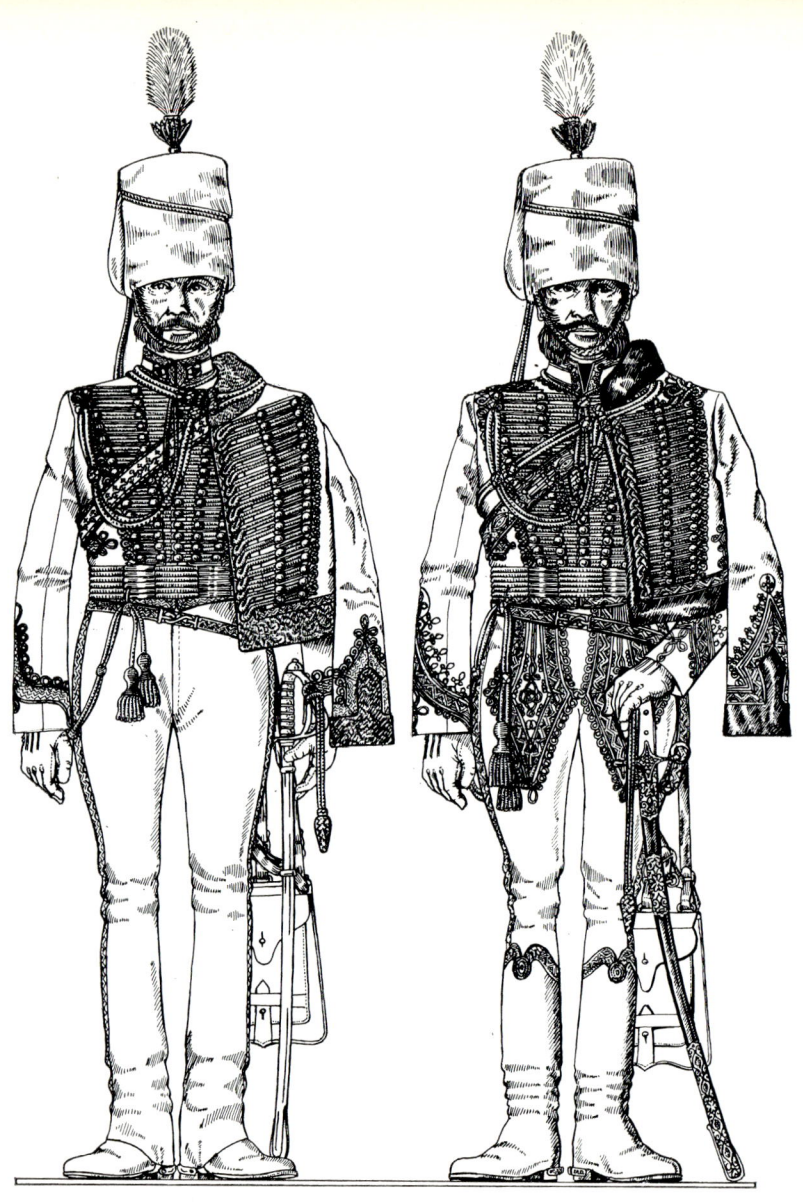

Hussar Officers, 1854. On the left an officer of the 8th Hussars in Full Dress and on the right an officer of the 11th Hussars in Levée Dress. The head-dress for both officers is the fur cap with white over red plume and scarlet bag for the 8th, and white over crimson plume and crimson bag for the 11th. Both jackets and pelisses are dark blue with gold lace and buttons. Dark blue overalls with a gold stripe were worn for the 8th and for the 11th crimson pantaloons were worn with gold lace and braid on the front. The feature of this dress was the Levée Dress sword. Most Hussar regiments had a special pattern sword of the Mameluke type for use with Levée Dress. In the case of the 11th the scabbard was black with gilt mountings.

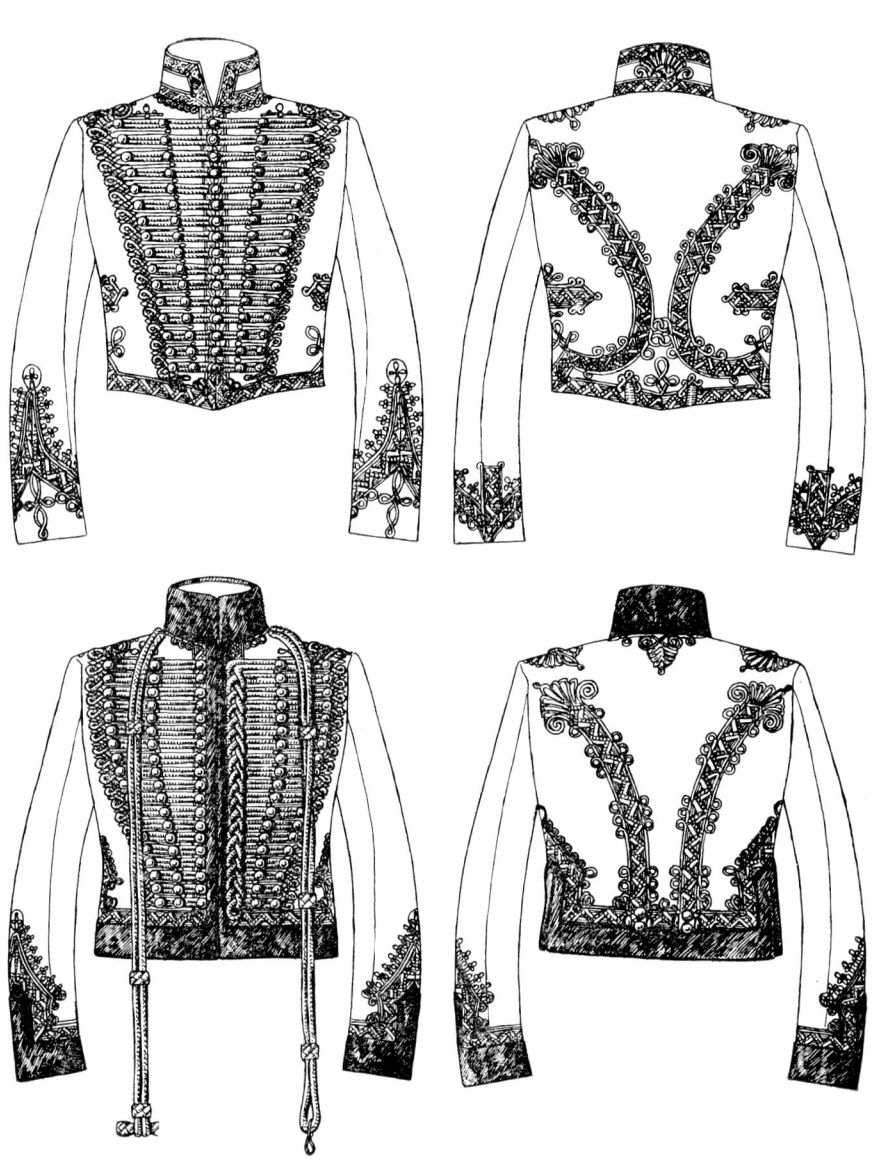

Officer's jacket and pelisse, 11th Hussars, 1854. These were the last patterns to be worn by the regiment before the introduction of the tunic. For each Hussar regiment at this time the manner in which the lace and braid was placed on these garments varied. Although all very elaborate the special feature for the 11th Hussars was the way in which the lace and tracing braid was placed on the cuffs. As can be seen on the drawing showing an officer of the 8th Hussars in Full Dress the less elaborate sleeve ornament and the jacket and pelisse lacked the decoration above. The top row of braid and at the back beneath the collar illustrate regimental differences.

with the white and yellow lace and embroidery being replaced by silver and gold.

This form of dress and horse furniture was worn until 1855 with the exception that when the 11th Light Dragoons were converted to Hussars in 1840 their new uniform consisted of a brown fur busby with crimson bag and white over crimson plume. A dark blue jacket and pelisse laced with gold, and crimson overalls (Fig 16), completed the uniform. For other ranks the uniform was similar to that of the officers but not so elaborate, with gold lace and cords for sergeants and yellow lace and cords for ranks below sergeant. A report by the Board of General officers dated June 1, 1845, states that the gold lace on the sergeants' dress and undress jackets and on the pelisse were now to be replaced by yellow worsted lace, only the Sergeant-Majors to retain their gold lace. Also in 1845 the number of buttons on the men's jackets and pelisses was reduced. Between 1845 and 1855 there was only three rows of buttons on the jacket and pelisse.

With the new regiment, the 11th Hussars, wearing a busby in place of the shako the 7th, 8th, and 10th regiments applied for permission to return to this type of head-dress and by 1842 all Hussar regiments, with the exception of the 15th, were wearing brown fur busbies with red bags and white over red plumes. The 11th kept their crimson colours and the 15th still retained their scarlet shakos up to 1855.

The final stages of this uniform which had made the British Hussar regiments the most handsomely dressed regiments of European Cavalry can be seen in Figures 15, 16, 17 and 18. The officer of the 8th Hussars (Fig 15) is in full dress. This gives the general appearance of an officer except for the regimental differences. An officer of the 11th (Fig 17) and a trooper of the 8th (Fig 18) shows the dress and equipment when with the 4th Light Dragoons, 13th Light Dragoons and 17th Lancers they formed the Light Brigade that took part in the famous Balaclava charge. The officer has the Pattern 1822, Light Cavalry Officer's sword while the trooper has the Pattern 1829, Light Cavalry Trooper's sword and carries a precussion carbine.

3: The Later Period: 1855-1914

DUE to the severe conditions of service during the Crimean War the clothing of the British Army was found to be totally unsuitable and the outcome of this was that the procuration of expensive and glamorous uniforms and horse furniture for the Hussars regiments was drastically changed. The short jacket and pelisse were replaced by a tunic and this new style of clothing remained with few alterations up to the start of the 1914-1918 War. The number of Hussar regiments at the close of the Crimean campaign was still five and a very detailed account of the clothing and horse furniture is given in the *Dress Regulations for the Army, 1857.*

The sections dealing with the Hussar regiments are given in full. It should be noted, however, that although the *Dress Regulations* states that the regulations must be scrupulously obeyed, they can only be considered as a guide to the general dress and appointments of each section of the army as many regiments were authorised to wear articles of regimental pattern. During the period 1855 to 1861 the number of Hussar regiments was gradually increased to thirteen, this number being reduced to twelve in 1897 when the 21st Hussars were converted to Lancers.

Dress Regulations for the Army 1857
Hussar Regiments

Distinctions of Rank
DRESS

Colonel	Crown and Star.
Lieutenant-Colonel	Crown
Major	Star.
Captain	Crown and Star.
Lieutenant	Crown.
Cornet	Star.

The rank badges are in silver embroidery worn on collar. For the Colonel, Lieutenant-Colonel and Major the collars are laced all round with gold lace, three quarters of an inch wide, a figured braiding within the lace. Sleeve ornament, knot of gold chain lace with figured braiding eight inches deep.

For Captains, collar laced round the top with gold lace and a figured braiding, Sleeve ornament, knot of gold chain lace and figured braiding eight inches deep.

For Lieutenants and Cornets, collar laced round the top with gold lace with a plain edging of gold braid within the lace, Sleeve ornament, knot of gold chain lace, edged with braid seven inches deep.

(These collar and cuff decorations as part of the rank distinctions were worn until 1902 when all officers then had to adopt the plain collar and cuffs as described for Lieutenants and Cornets).

UNDRESS

Field Officers (Colonel, Lieutenant-Colonel and Major). Relative badges in gold embroidery on collar. Other Ranks (Captain, Lieutenant and Cornet), no badges to be worn.

DRESS

Jacket—Tunic, entirely of blue cloth; single breasted; the collar two inches high, rounded in front. On each side of the breast, six loops of gold chain lace, with caps and drops, fastening with six gold worked olivets; the top loop eight inches long, the bottom one four inches. The jacket edged all round (except the collar) with gold chain lace. On the back seams a double chain of the same lace, edged with braid forming three eyes at the top, passing under a netted cap at the waist and terminating in a knot at bottom of skirt. Waist long, the skirt nine inches deep for an officer five feet nine inches in height, with a variation of half an inch for every inch of diffierence in the height of the wearer, the skirt lined with black. Cuffs ten and a half inches round.

Waistcoat—Scarlet, with half ball buttons and ornamented with gold cord (not worn in the 8th or 11th Hussars).

Cap—Busby, black sable fur, falling half an inch below the body or framework of the cap. Outside measurement, front seven and three quarter inches, sides eight inches, back nine inches, top nine sixteenths less than bottom; front half inch out of perpendicular, back, capped to fit the head; a gold gimp oval cockade, two inches long, one and a half inches broad in centre of front, fixed on a level with the top edge of the cap. Gilt ring for line fixed at top of right side of cap underneath the fly; gilt hook at top of right side to hook up the chain. Spring socket in centre of front for plume. Fly or bag, cloth, crimson in the 11th, scarlet for other regiments. Seam in front covered with a line of gold figuring braid and a single line of gold figuring braid down the centre. At the point of juncture a gold gimp one inch button.

Cap Chain—Dead and bright gold corded, fixed to the left side by an eye or loop and attachable to right side by a hook.

Cap Lines—Gold pearl cord, with sliders and olive ends to match, encircling the cap three times and worn round the neck.

Plume—Eight inches high above the cap, encircled by a gold ring.

7th Regiment, entire white osprey feathers.

8th Regiment, the same, but lower third covered with red feathers.

10th Regiment, the same, but lower third covered with black feathers.

11th Regiment, the same, but lower third covered with crimson feathers.

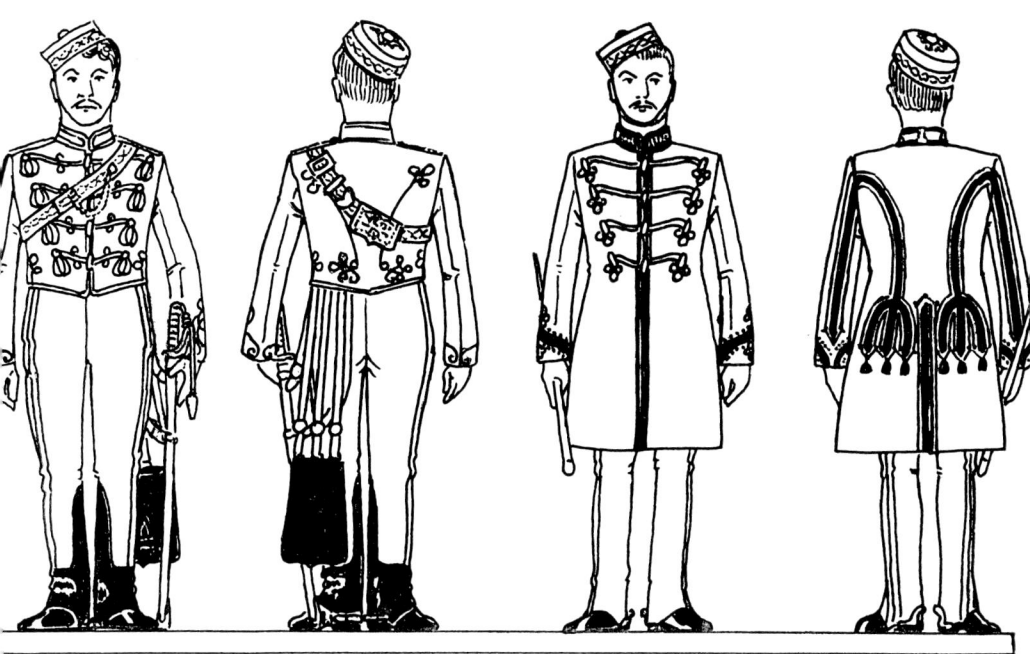

ABOVE: Officers of the 11th Hussars, 1864. The dress shown on the left is the stable jacket. This was dark blue with gold braid on the front, collar and cuffs. The booted overalls were crimson and the round forage cap was crimson with a band of gold lace. The top of this cap was embroidered in gold tracing cord. The frock coat was dark blue with black mohair braid and cords.

15th Regiment, entire scarlet osprey feathers.

Plume socket — Gilt corded ball, with four upright leaves.

Stock—Black silk.

Trousers—Dress, blue cloth (crimson for the 11th), stripe of gold regimental lace one inch and a half wide down outer seam.

Boots — Wellington.

Spurs — Yellow metal, crane neck, two inches long.

Sword — Steel mounted, half basket hilt, with two fluted bars on the outside, black fish skin grip bound with silver wire, the blade slightly curved, thirty five and a half inches long and one and a quarter wide, with a round back, terminating within eleven inches of the point.

Scabbard — Steel, with a large shoe at the bottom, solid band and rings, a trumpet formed mouth.

Sword Knot — Gold and crimson, with a large acorn.

Sword Belt — Gold lace, one inch and a quarter wide, with scarlet morocco edging and lining, fastened in front with a clasp ornament; gilt mountings, and three rings, from which hang two sword slings of similar widths, with loops and buckles for rings of scabbard, and three half inch tache-slings with loops and buckles for rings of sabretache. The belt to be worn under the jacket.

Sabretache — Scarlet cloth face, laced with gold lace, two and a quarter inches wide, leaving an edge of scarlet, embroidered regimental badge in the centre, three gilt rings at the top, pocket scarlet morocco; slings short enough to prevent sabretache from hanging below the calf of the leg.

Pouch Belt—Gold lace, one inch and a half wide, scarlet cloth edging and morocco lining, gilt ornamented buckle, tip and slide; attached to sides of pouch. The 10th Hussars are permitted to wear in both dress and undress a pouch and pouch belt of black patent leather, according to regimental patterns.

Pouch Box — Scarlet cloth, circular flap, five inches deep, six inches wide at top, six and a half at bottom, edged round with gold braid and embroidery, embroidered regimental badge in centre.

In the 11th Hussars the cloth face and morocco pocket of the sabretache, and the lining and edging of the belts were crimson instead of scarlet, and a pouch box is sanctioned, of gilt metal with silver ornaments, according to regimental pattern.

Gloves — White leather.

UNDRESS

Frock — Blue cloth, single breasted, with six flat braided loops and four rows of olivets on the breast, stand up collar eged with flat braid, and with figuring inside; sleeves, braid extending from edge of cuff ten inches towards the elbow; back and skirt braided with broad and narrow braid and with olivets and tassels, lined with black silk and with relative collar badges for Field Officers.

Trousers — Blue cloth (crimson for 11th) with a pale yellow stripe, one inch and a half wide down the outward seam, and strapped with patent leather.

Forage Cap — Blue cloth for the 7th, 8th and 10th regiments, crimson cloth for the 11th and scarlet for the 15th, a gold band of regimental lace, same as worn on dress trousers, one inch and three quarters wide, a gold braided ornament and purl button at top, the seam of the crown of the cap encircled with gold braid; without peak.

Shell Jacket — Blue, single breasted, with olivets and gold lace according to regimental pattern and relative badges of rank for Field Officers.

Spurs — Steel, crane necked, two inches long.

Sword knot — Of regimental pattern.

Sabretache, Belt, Pouch and Pouch Belt of black patent leather, with gilt mountings.

Great Coat and Cape, blue cloth lined with scarlet for the 7th, 10th and 15th regiments, white for the 8th, and crimson for the 11th.

Regimental Staff

The Adjutant and Riding Master to wear the uniform of their rank.

The Paymaster, Quarter-Master, Surgeon, Assistant Surgeon and Veterinary Surgeon to wear the same uniform as the other officers, except that they wear the cocked hat, with gold bullion tassels, and loop one and three eighths inch wide, formed of four rows of gold gimp chain, with regimental button.

The Quarter-Master to wear a white feather drooping five inches. The Surgeon, Assistant Surgeon and Veterinary Officer to wear a feather of black cock's-tail of same pattern.

The Surgeon and Assistant Surgeon to wear a black Morocco shoulder

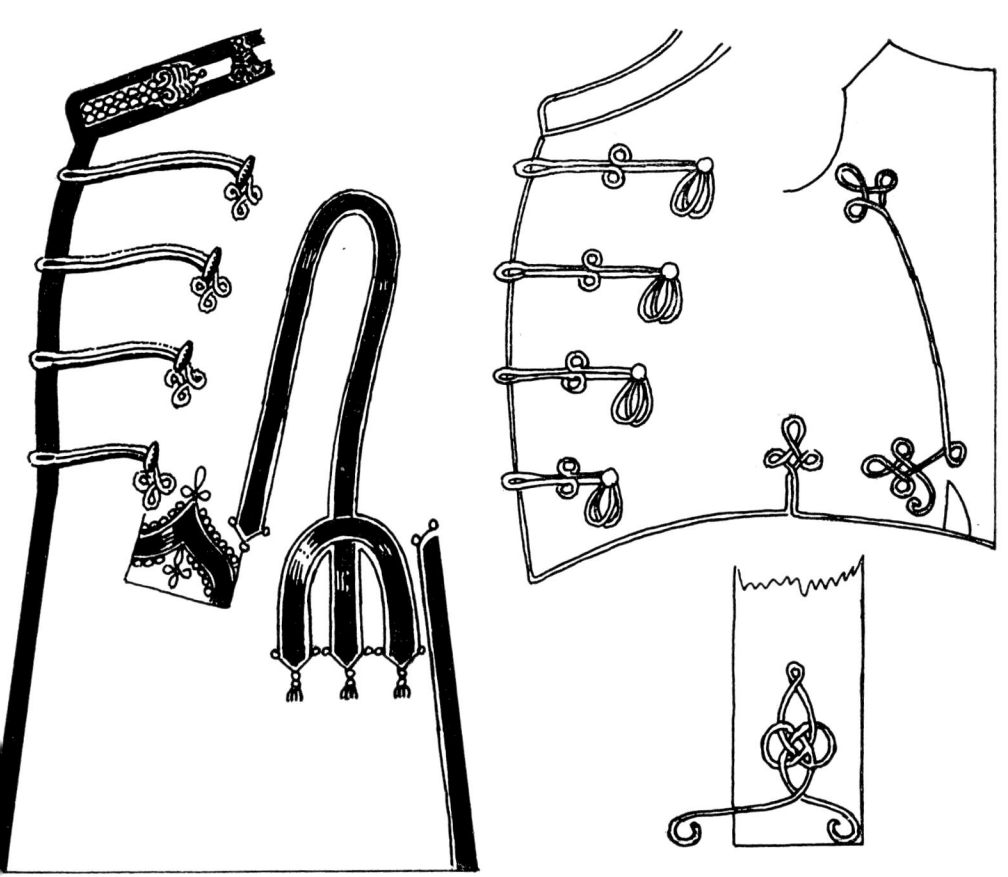

ABOVE: The frock coat and stable jacket as worn by officers of the 11th Hussars, 1864. The details were copied from sketches made by a military tailor. The two garments compare well with contemporary illustrations although artists indicate a slight wave in the rows of lace across the front of the stable jacket.

belt with a small case for instruments, instead of the regimental pouch and belt.

Paymasters to wear no feathers.

Horse Furniture of Cavalry Officers Dress Regulations, 1857

Saddle — Hussar brown hogskin, brass head and cantle; Hussar stirrup leathers and irons, blue girths.

Bridle — Brown leather, with brass wire whole buckles, bent branch bit, with pads, and plain bent bar link and tee bridoon; plain leather head collar, bit-head, and bridoon rein sewn on, regimental bosses on bit, and face piece. Hussar regiments to have hair throat ornaments, of regimental colours, eighteen inches long, with brass ball and socket.

Chain — Steel.

Breastplate — Brown leather, with brass wire, whole buckles, and regimental boss, on stitched leather heart.

Crupper — Brown leather single strap, with regimental boss, and buckles as before.

Surcingle and Shabraque strap — Brown leather.

Dress Lambskin—Black Ukraine lambskin, three feet four inches long, thirteen and a half inches in depth, lined moleskin, trimmed scarlet cloth.

Undress Lambskin — Black Ukraine lambskin with leather seat and large flap to open for wallets, lined moleskin, trimmed secarlet cloth. The 7th and 10th Hussars are permitted to wear the leopard's skins in lieu of the Lambskin.

Valise — Blue cloth, twenty seven inches long, hollowed to centre, ends six and a half inches in diameter, embroidered with Arabic number and relative regimental initial letters.

Shabraques
Dress Regulations, 1857

Hussar Regiments — To be of blue cloth, cut with a peak behind, and squared off in front, four feet four inches in length, three feet one inch in depth, trimmed gold overall lace, lined moleskin.

7th Hussars. To have on fore corners, V.R. and crown in gold, on hind corners, crown over Sphinx, then scroll (Prince Albert's Own Queen's Own) round it, and 7H under it, all gold.

8th Hussars. To have on fore corners, V.R., and crown in gold, on hind corners, crown over harp, then scroll with motto (Pristinæ Virtutis Memores) with 8H under it, all gold except harp strings, silver.

10th Hussars. To have on fore corners. V.R., and crown in gold, on hind corners, crown over plume, with coronet and (Ich Dien) within scroll (Prince of Wales's Own) enclosing 10 and H under it. Plume in silver, rest in gold.

11th Hussars. To have on fore corners, V.R., and crown in gold, on hind corners, crown over Sphinx, then scroll (Prince Albert's Own Hussars) enclosing 11 and H under it. Sphinx silver embroidery, rest gold.

15th Hussars. To have on fore corners, V.R., and crown in gold, on hind corners' crown and Queen's crest, within garter with the word (Merebimur) round it, then crossed flags reversed, and 15H under it, flags in silver, rest in gold embroidery.

THE first of the additional Hussar regiments was the 18th. This was a new regiment raised in 1858 and the unusual feature of the uniform was in the colour of the busby bag and plume which were Lincoln green (Fig 19). This colour was used until 1878 when the busby bag was changed to dark blue and the plume to white over a scarlet base.

The next three regiments were the Bengal European Cavalry regiments

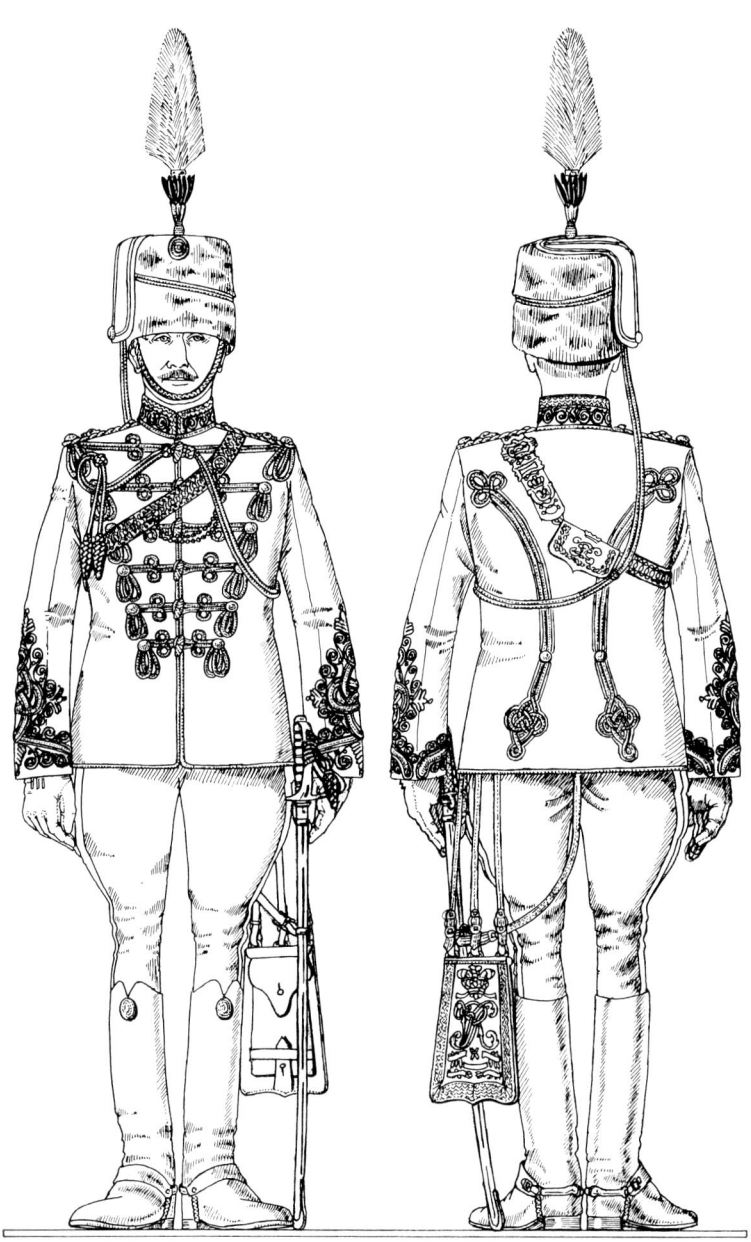

Officers' Full Dress, 1895. The uniform was the same for officers of all Hussar regiments except for the regimental differences. In the case of the 10th these were the unusual way in which the busby lines were passed under the left arm instead of around the neck, the caps at the ends of the top row of tunic lace placed on the ends of the shoulder cords, the sword of 1822 Light Cavalry pattern, and the very distinctive pouch and pouch belt. In Levée Dress the 10th Hussar officers wore scarlet pantaloons and Hessian boots which had a narrow band of gold lace round the top edge ending with a gold boss in front.

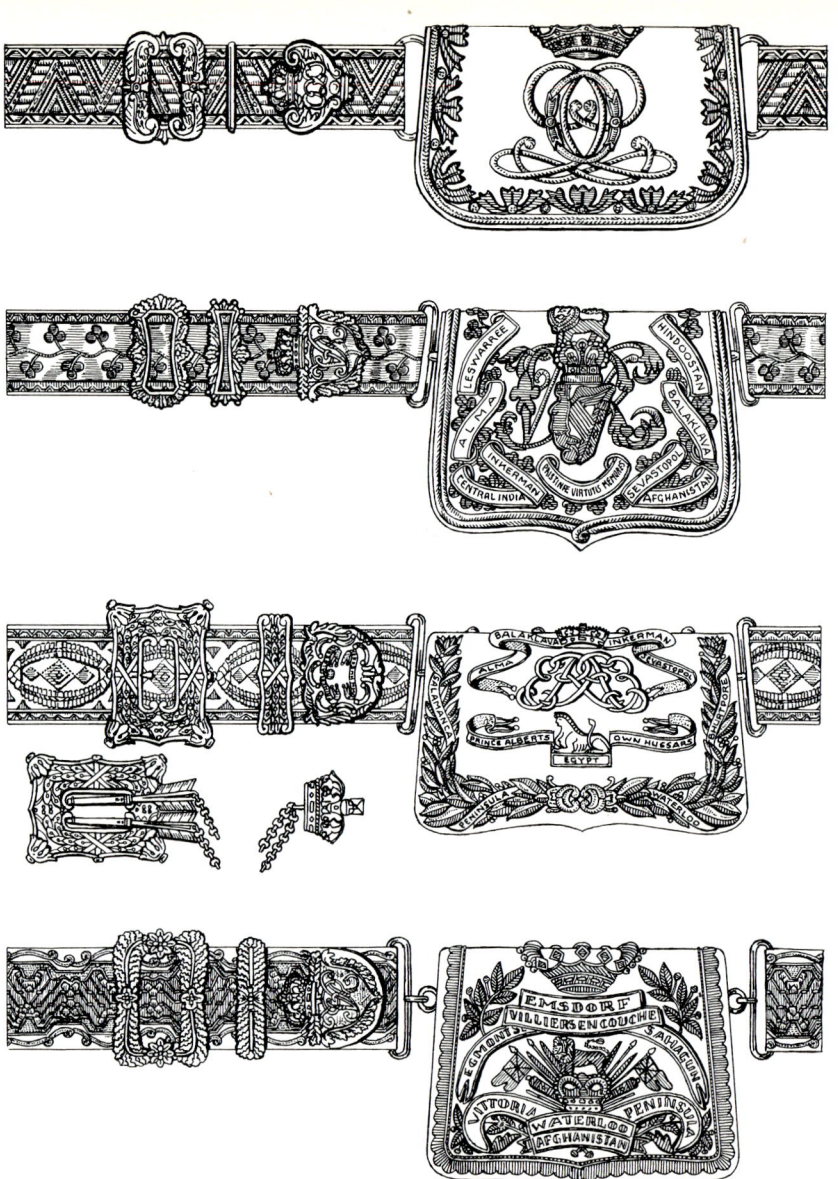

of the Honourable East India Company's army and after the Mutiny these three regiments were placed on the British establishment as Light Dragoons but were quickly converted to Hussars having the numbers 19, 20, and 21. The 19th had a white plume and busby bag, the 20th had a crimson plume and bag, the plume being changed in 1894 for one of yellow, while the 21st had a French grey bag and a white plume.

In 1861 the four remaining Light Dragoon regiments were converted to Hussars. As Light Dragoons these regiments had collars and cuffs of

OPPOSITE PAGE:

TOP: Officer's pouch and pouch belt ornaments, 7th Hussars. The pouch was of red cloth embroidered in gold and edged with a gold tracing cord. The belt was gold laced edged with red. and had a gilt ornamental buckle, tip and slide at the back.

SECOND FROM TOP: Officer's pouch and pouch belt ornaments, 8th Hussars. These were faced with red cloth. The central design was a gold crown and lion over a gold harp, the harp strings being silver. This was all placed over the cypher 'V.R.', which was embroidered in silver. The rest of the embroidery and lace was gold with the lettering on the honour scrolls in silver wire. The belt was laced with gold of regimental pattern bearing a shamrock design and had a gilt buckle, tip and slide on the back.

THIRD FROM TOP: Officer's pouch and pouch belt ornaments, 11th Hussars. The pouch itself was made of crimson leather but was very unusual in that the flap was made of brass. All the decoration on the pouch flap was silver. The pouch belt was gold laced, edged crimson and, as with the pouch, all the ornaments were silver.

BOTTOM: Officer's pouch and pouch belt ornaments, 15th Hussars. The colours for the pouch closely follow those for the sabretache, being all gold embroidered except for the sword blades and pike heads which are silver and all on a scarlet cloth face. The pouch belt was gold laced and had a gilt buckle tip and slide, the lace on this belt was edged with tracing cord on a scarlet ground.

---

regimental facing colour, these being scarlet for the 3rd, 4th, and 14th and buff for the 13th. On conversion the 3rd and 13th were allowed to retain their facings on the collar; for the 3rd the busby bag was Garter blue and the plume white, for the 4th a yellow bag and scarlet plume and for the 13th a buff bag and white plume. The buff colour of the bag was in fact white. The last regiment, the 14th, had a yellow bag and a white plume. This uniform with a few minor changes remained in use until 1914. The big change in appearance was affected by 1902 when the sabretache and shabraque were abolished. Figures 25 to 36 show officers in Full Dress and Review Order shortly before these items were abolished. They are all wearing the old type plume which was replaced in 1901 by the type shown in Figures 41 and 44. The officer's pouches are described in the 1874 Dress Regulations as follows:

3rd. Black leather, silver flap, gilt ornaments.
4th. Black leather, silver flap, gilt ornaments.
7th. Scarlet cloth, embroidered in gold.
8th. Scarlet cloth, embroidered in gold.
10th. Black patent leather, special pattern.
11th. Black leather, gilt metal flap, silver ornaments.
13th. Black leather, silver flap, gilt ornaments.
14th. Black leather, silver flap, gilt ornaments.
15th. Scarlet cloth, embroidered in gold.
18th. Scarlet leather, embroidered in gold.
19th. Black leather, silver flap, gilt ornaments.
20th. Black leather, silver flap, gilt ornaments.
21st. Black leather, silver flap, gilt ornaments.

The pattern for the 3rd, 4th, 13th, 14th, 19th, 20th and 21st with a silver flap was the old Light Dragoon pattern. The pouch belts for the 7th, 8th and 15th did not have chains and prickers on the front. The figures represent officers below the rank of Captain. For all officers the rank

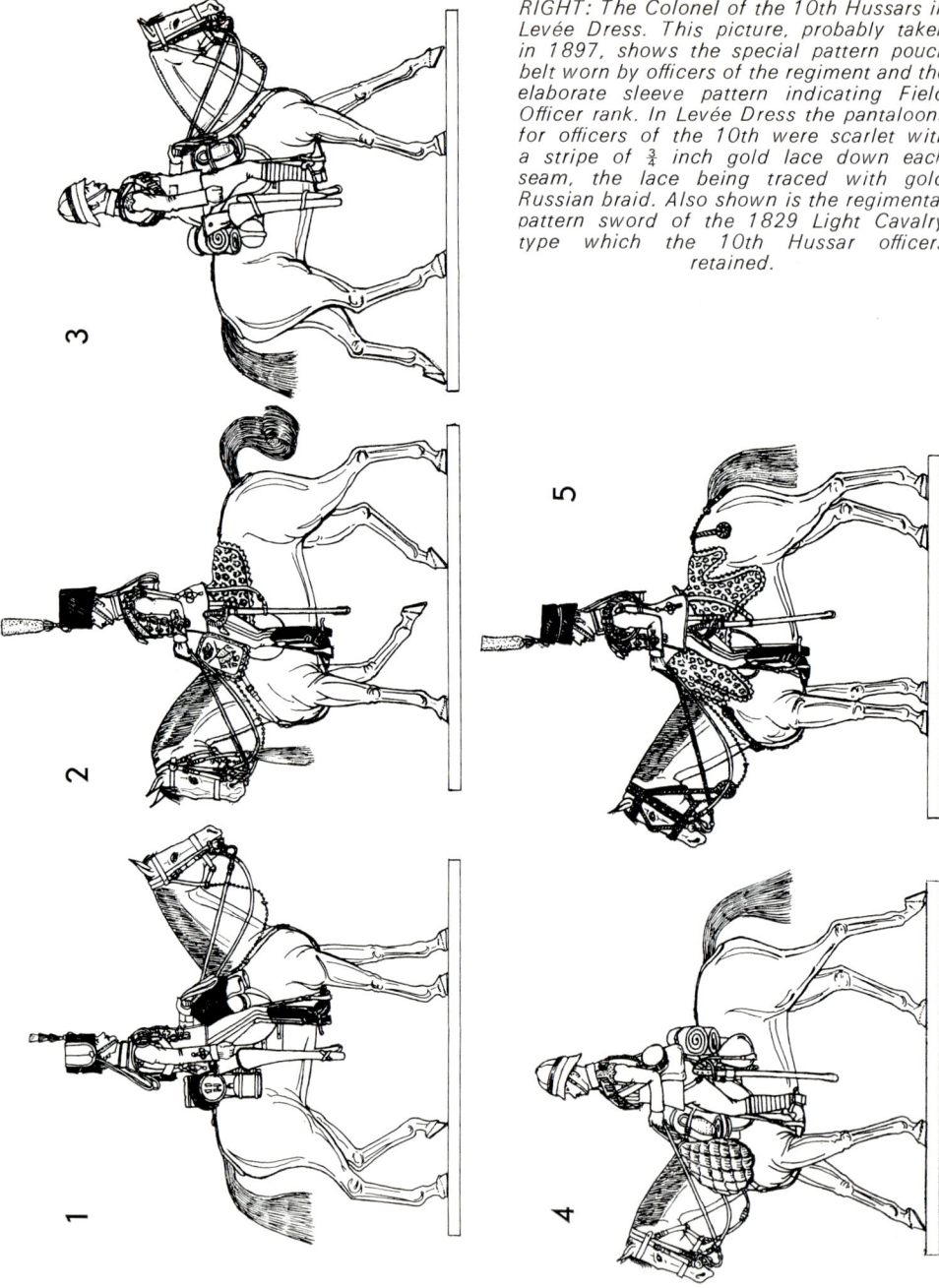

RIGHT: The Colonel of the 10th Hussars in Levée Dress. This picture, probably taken in 1897, shows the special pattern pouch belt worn by officers of the regiment and the elaborate sleeve pattern indicating Field Officer rank. In Levée Dress the pantaloons for officers of the 10th were scarlet with a stripe of ¾ inch gold lace down each seam, the lace being traced with gold Russian braid. Also shown is the regimental pattern sword of the 1829 Light Cavalry type which the 10th Hussar officers retained.

RIGHT:
A Captain of the 3rd Hussars
in Review Order, 1898. The
row of eyes on the collar and
round the Austrian knot sleeve
ornament indicates rank as well
as the two stars on each shoulder strap. It was not until 1904
that the rank of Captain was
indicated by three stars.

OPPOSITE PAGE:
1. A trooper of the 11th Hussars, 1895. This figure is representative of
all regiments at this period and illustrates the method used to place items
of equipment. The cloak was folded and placed across the wallets beneath
the black sheepskin. The mess tin was strapped above the valise and the
water canteen placed just below the valise on the off side.
2. An officer of the 15th Hussars after the shabraque and sabretache
were abolished, the device on the front of the leopard skin was distinctive
to the 15th. In general appearance, allowing for regimental differences,
this was the full dress pattern for all Hussar officers until 1914.
3. A Hussar trooper, 1900, off side. All Cavalry regiments proceeding to
South Africa were issued with a regulation pattern saddlery. The clothing
was khaki and spare items of clothing and equipment were fixed to the
saddle. In this view can be seen the mess tin, spare boot and carbine.
4. A Hussar trooper, 1900, near side. The trooper wears his bandolier
over the left shoulder and over the right shoulder are the straps for the
haversack and water bottle which are placed at the left hip. The sword is
carried in a frog attached to the front of the saddle.
5. An officer of the 10th Hussars, 1914. The regiment still retained the
cowrie shell ornament on the leatherwork and had a full leopard skin
covering the saddle, this represents the final full dress before the 1914-18
War.

A Corporal of the 14th Hussars in Review Order. The badge usually referred to as a Sergeants arm badge was worn by all NCOs and Sergeants in the 14th Hussars. It can be seen above the chevrons on the right arm. The horse's bridle and bit were introduced about 1885, all the leather being brown with brass buckles. The head rope was white. The corporal is holding a Martini Henry carbine.

indication worn on the collar and cuffs as shown in the colour plate illustrating these items was in use until 1902 when the system was changed. The change was that from 1902 until 1914 officers of all ranks had the same pattern collar and cuff ornament, this being the collar laced round the top and front edges only and the cuffs having the single Austrian knot as shown for Lieutenants.

For parades other than Full Dress and Review order there were forms

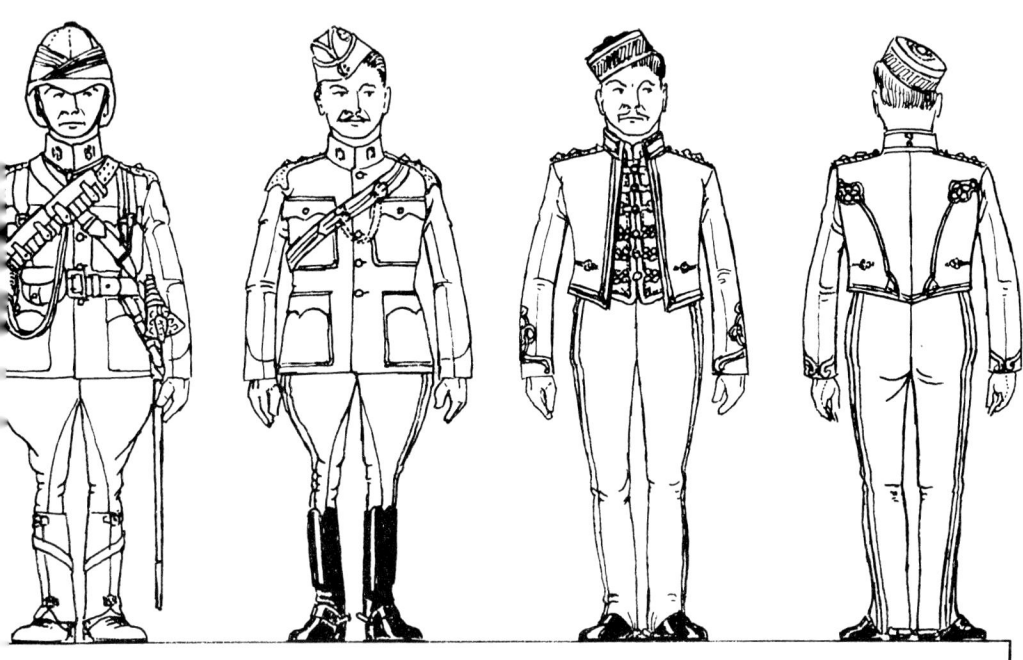

ABOVE: The first figure shows the uniform and equipment worn at the start of the South African War. The clothing was of a light shade of khaki. The belts and bandolier were brown leather and the haversack strap was khaki webbing. The second figure shows the frock of the pattern sealed in 1898. It is all dark blue except for the 3rd who had a scarlet collar and the 13th whose collar was buff. This garment had steel shoulder chains and gilt buttons. The field cap was scarlet for all regiments except the 11th, who had crimson, and the 13th who had a white cap with blue flaps. The welts and seams of the field cap were traced with gold cord. The figure on the right shows stable jacket, and mess vest in wear. Detailed drawings are shown later in the book.

of undress such as the stable jacket shown in Fig 42 and the blue serge frock as in Fig 43. With these orders of dress only the plain black sabretache was used.

In 1880 the system whereby officers' rank badges were placed on the ends of the collar was replaced by a system which removed the badges from the collar and placed them on shoulder cords. For the Colonel, Lieutenant Colonel and Major the badges remained the same but for Captains there were now only two stars, for Lieutenants there was one and there was no rank badge for Second Lieutenants. For Warrant Officers, Sergeant and NCOs the badge of rank was worn on the right arm. With the badges was worn a distinctive regimental badge, this usually being referred to as a Sergeant's arm badge, made of silver and worn by ranks above corporal. With the exception of the 14th Hussars, this badge was worn above the chevrons and if an additional trade or rank badge was worn it was placed above the chevrons but below the additional badge. These badges can be seen on Figures 37 and 47. The Regulations for the Supply of Clothing and Necessities to the Regular

ABOVE:
The Regimental Quartermaster Sergeant of the 11th Hussars. His badge of rank was worn on the right arm below the elbow and consisted of an eight pointed star above four inverted gold chevrons. The regimental pattern sergeant's arm badge was placed between the star and chevrons. This photograph shows clearly the horse furniture and the blanket and numnah pad placed beneath the saddle.

OPPOSITE PAGE:
A trooper in Review Order, 1897. The photograph shows clearly how the sword scabbard was placed in a frog on the saddle and the manner in which the girth was strapped and buckled. The bridle and saddlery were of the Universal pattern with a white head rope.

ABOVE: A comparison of the officers' full dress uniform before and after the order discontinuing the wearing of the sabretache. The officer on the left belongs to the 8th Hussars and he wears the Hussar type pouch belt and pouch while the officer of the 3rd Hussars on the right has a belt and pouch of Light Dragoon pattern with silver chains and prickers on the front and a silver mounted pouch.

Forces, dated September 24, 1887, states that these badges will not be worn by Warrant Officers and gives the following details for these special badges:

3rd Hussars. White Horse, worn by Staff Sergeants, Sergeants and Kettle Drummer.

4th Hussars (not given in this regulation). Superimposed on the monogram 'Q.O.H.', a crown, with IV below and at the base a scroll with the motto 'Mente et Manu'.

7th Hussars (not given). The regimental monogram 'Q.O.,' reversed and intertwined being surmounted by a crown, this badge had a backing of red cloth.

8th Hussars. Harp and crown, worn by Staff Sergeants and Sergeants.

10th Hussars. Prince of Wales's Plumes, worn by Staff Sergeants and Sergeants.

11th Hussars. Crest and Motto of HRH the late Prince Consort, worn by Staff Sergeants and Sergeants.

13th Hussars. This regiment did not wear the special arm badge.

14th Hussars. Prussian Eagle, this regiment was an exception in that the arm badge was worn by all ranks from Lance Corporal to Staff Sergeant. For Lance Corporals and Corporals the badge was made from German silver and for Sergeants and Staff Sergeants from Sterling silver.

15th Hussars. Royal Crest.

18th Hussars: (not given). Monogram 'Q.M.O.,' in silver.

19th Hussars. Elephant, worn by Staff Sergeants and Sergeants.

20th Hussars. Arm badge not worn.

21st Hussars: (not given). A photograph which show's the regimental band wearing the blue serge undress tunic and another in which a Staff Sergeant is shown do not reveal any special badges being worn above the chevrons. Another photograph showing a troop in the new Lancer uniform when the regiment was converted shows a Sergeant with no special badge above the chevrons but by 1905 the 21st Lancers Staff Sergeants and Sergeants were wearing a badge of the cypher 'V.R.I.,' and crown. Although regulations state that these badges were not to be worn by Warrant Officers this was not strictly adhered to.

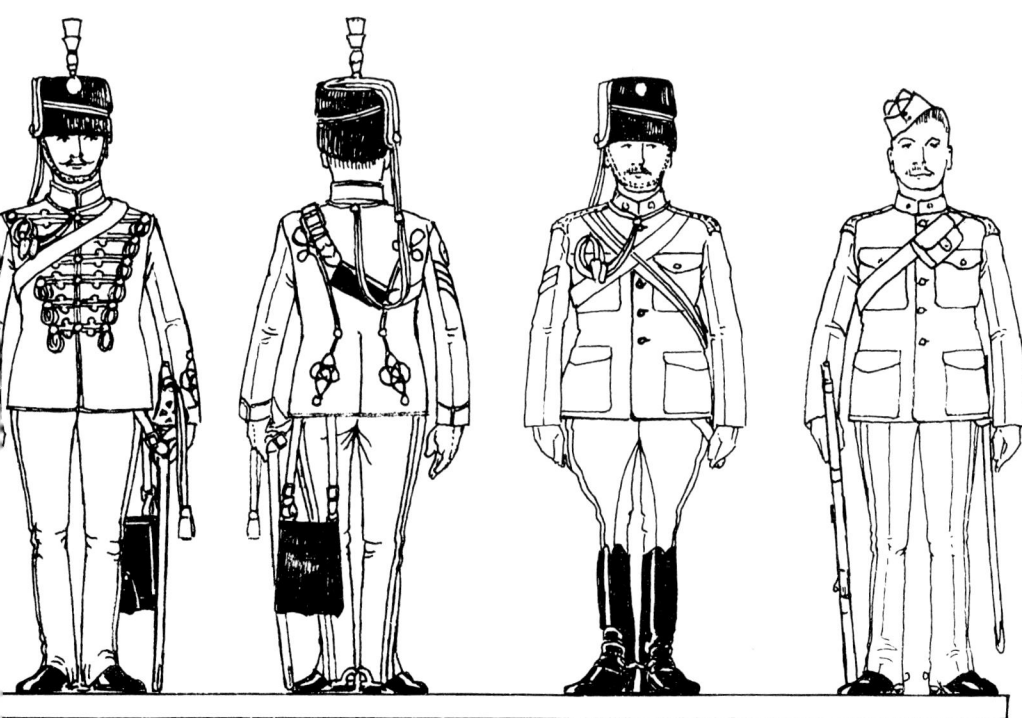

ABOVE: The two figures on the left show the dress worn on full dress dismounted parades up to 1900. The third figure is wearing the dress worn on field days at the end of the nineteenth century. The jacket was dark blue with a collar patch of the facing colour for the 3rd and 13th Hussars. The fourth figure shows the dismounted drill order for the same period. The folding field cap was worn with this dress.

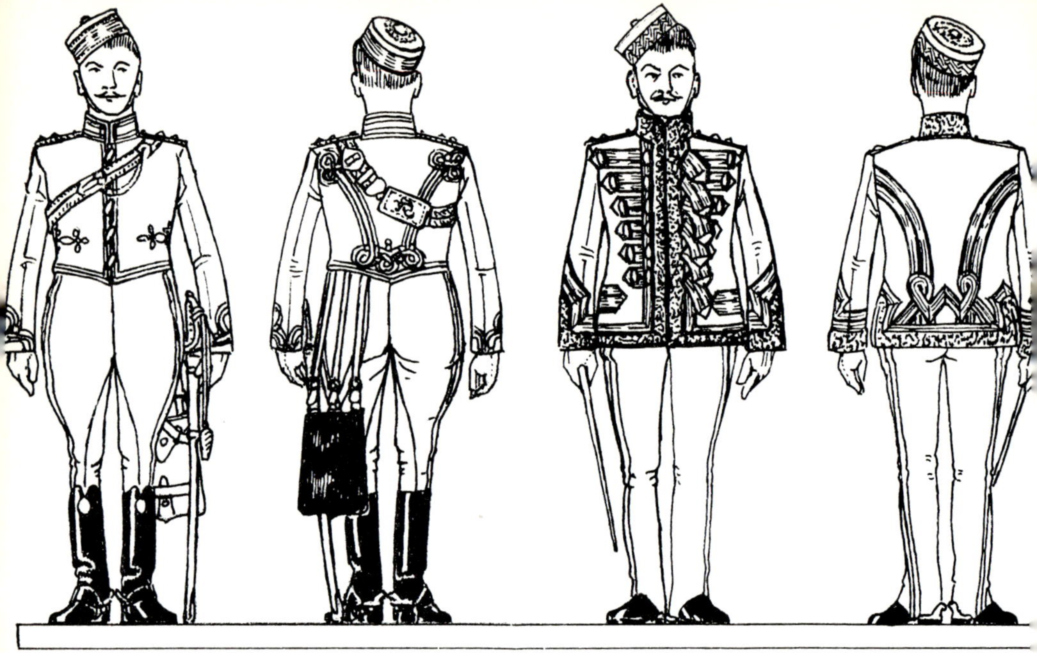

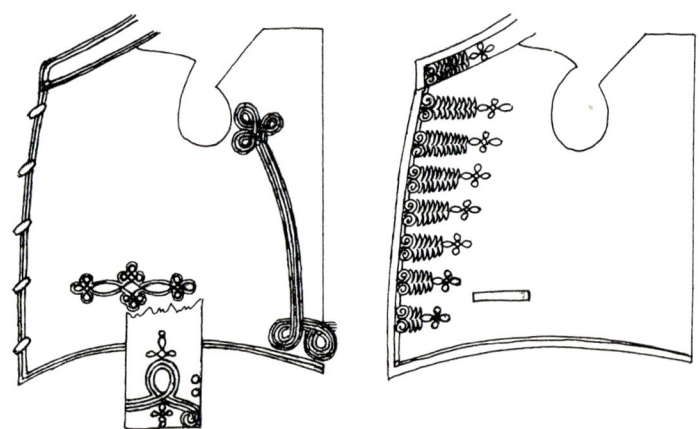

ABOVE: The stable jackets and patrol jackets illustrated in detail on other pages can be seen in these figures, the officer on the left represents the 3rd Hussars, the officer on the right the 4th Hussars.

ABOVE: 4th Hussars. The stable jacket on the left is all dark blue. The notes on the original sketch note no shoulder cords. Sleeves, side seams and collar were edged with gold wire cord. Tracing cord was carried on the collar, inside all edges and cuffs, the pockets being noted as all tracer and the cord on the back seams as being traced in and out. The vest is edged with gold lace and is decorated with a pattern of gold tracing cord. The collar ornament is marked four inches long, the top row on the vest as four and a half inches, and the bottom row as two and a half inches long.

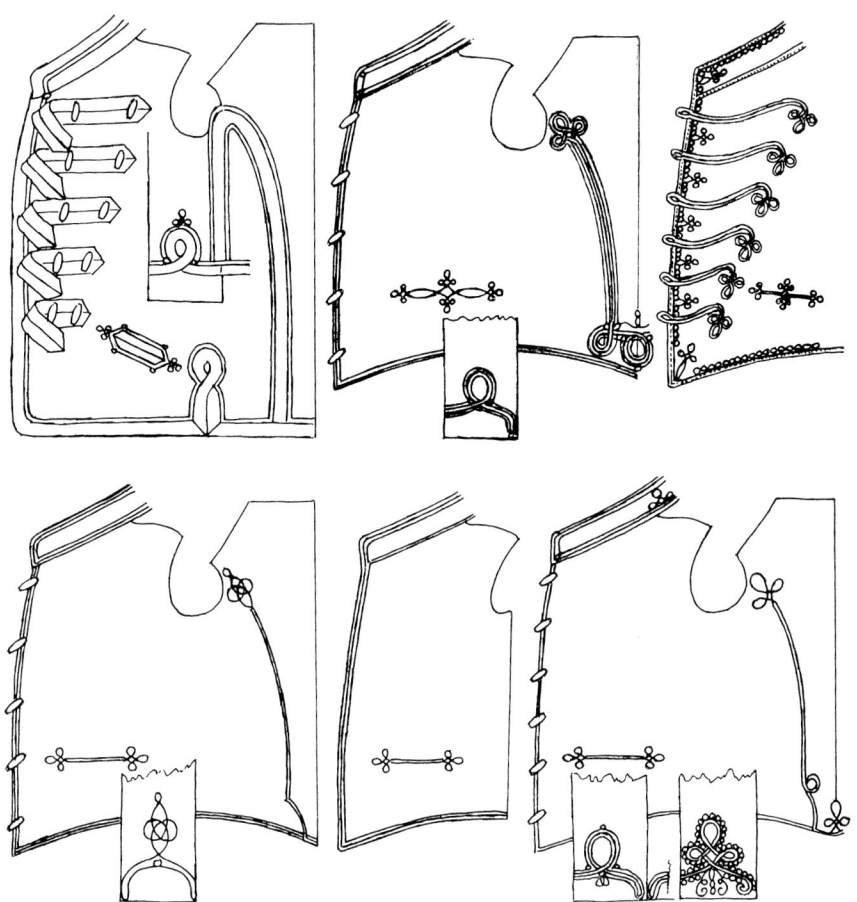

TOP ROW: 3rd Hussars. Copied from contemporary tailor's sketches the patrol jacket on the left is dark blue edged and faced with black mohair lace and trimmed with black mohair cord. A note on the original sketch gives the date as 1880-1886 and is marked cancelled 1887. The central garment is the stable jacket, dark blue with a scarlet collar, the collar, cuffs and back seams and edges trimmed with gold cord and lined with tracing cord. The mess vest shown on the right is marked—scarlet. It had olivets up the right side, and gimp loops. The gold gimp lace edging went all round the vest including the lower edge of the collar. The rest of the decoration was gold tracing cord. Both the stable jacket and mess vest are dated December 1887.

BOTTOM ROW: 7th Hussars, stable jacket. All dark blue trimmed with gold. A note states that the jacket was lined with drab. The vest shown in the centre is scarlet. Notes on the drawing give two rows of gold Russian cord on the edge, showing a quarter inch scarlet light between. Russian cord on collar, seam and no studs down front edge. The drawings are marked 1884. A patrol jacket is shown among the original drawings, dated 1884. It is the same as the pattern for 1900. For the 8th Hussars on the right, the stable jacket is dark blue. The drawing is marked as edged with gold square cord, the collar trimmed inside the square cord with tracing braid. The sleeve ornament for Captains and Lieutenants is shown on the left and the Field Officers on the right. The cuffs are marked close traced.

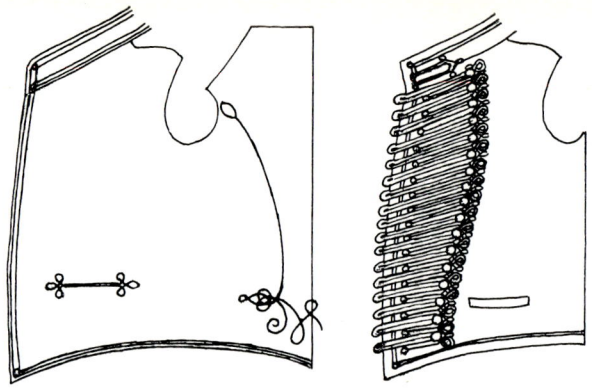

ABOVE: 10th Hussars, stable jacket and mess vest. The stable jacket is all dark blue edged with gold cord and traced so that a light of dark blue shows between the cord and tracing. The jacket was closed with hooks and eyes. The vest is marked to be scarlet, with hooks and eyes to the throat, three rows of buttons, one ball and two half-ball. The lace and cords are gold, the drawings are marked for Lt Onslow, March 1889.

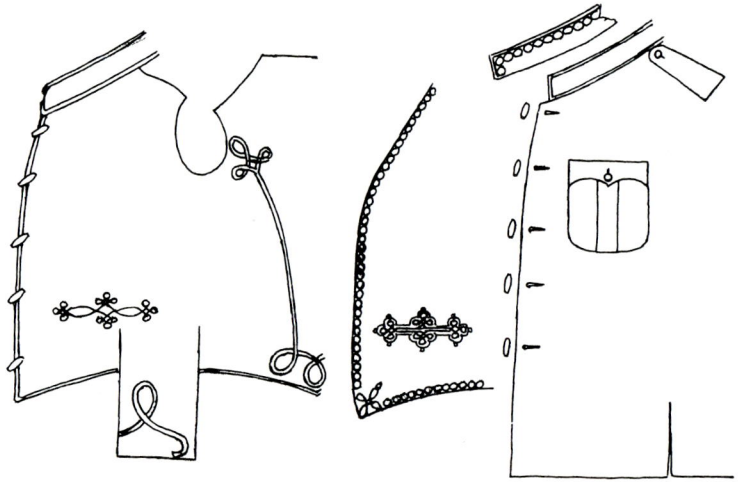

ABOVE: 14th Hussars. The tailor's sketches for the two garments illustrated date the stable jacket as October 1883 and the mess vest as March 1883. The stable jacket is all dark blue. The notes for this give gold wire Russian on side seams and edges, traced all round. The Austrian knot on the sleeve to be traced underneath. The vest is marked to be scarlet, all lace and tracing gold. A sketch of a patrol jacket dated 1879 shows the same pattern as worn in 1900. Two other garments noted are for December 1879. A thin patrol jacket made to the new regular cavalry pattern. All corners to be made square except the front which is to be rounded. The sleeves are the same as the frock. September 1883 is the date for the Serge patrol jacket. It was to have no lining, five holes and buttons, buttons plain and no shoulder cords. The sleeves and collar were as for the shell jacket. Note the two breast patch pockets.

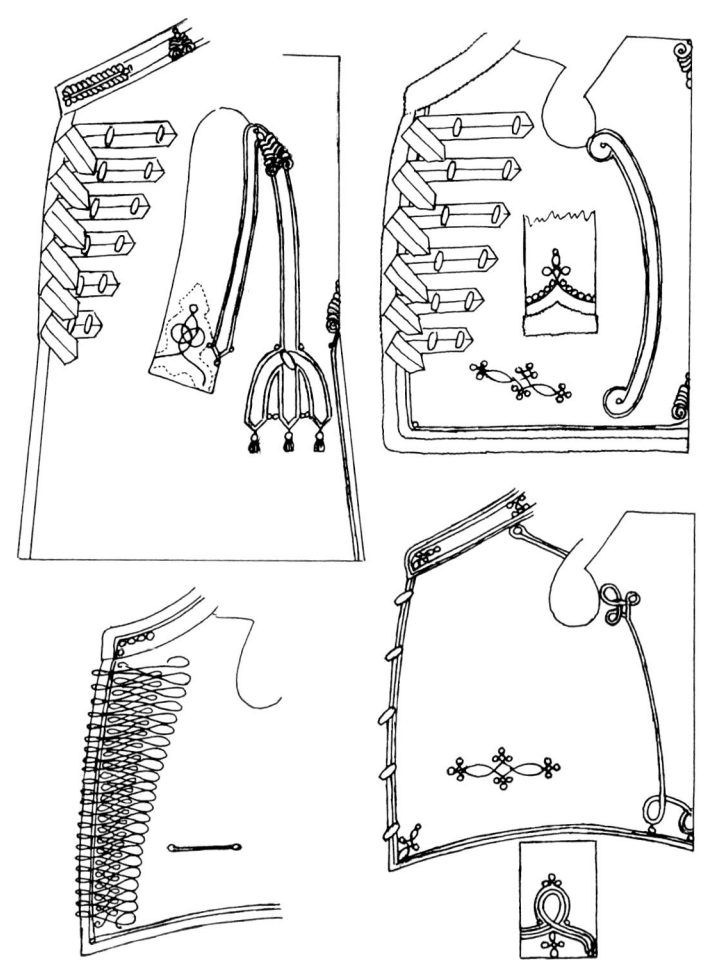

ABOVE: 13th Hussars. Top left is a frock coat, all dark blue with black mohair lace and cords. A feature of this coat is the ornamental design on the collar, the top of the back seams and the back slit. The cuffs are marked as Field Officers, full dress pattern, but in black cord. Top right is a patrol jacket, all dark blue with black braid and cord. The collar, cuffs and edges were trimmed with black astrakhan. The cuff decoration is noted as five inches high. Bottom left is a mess vest. The notes on the original drawing explain this garment as being buff, five eighths inch gold lace on edge, gold gimp loops traced to show no light, five eyes only on collar, the other parts traced. Bottom right is a stable jacket, all dark blue except the collar which is marked buff. The jacket was trimmed with gold cord and tracer. The cord on the shoulders is marked straight.
All original drawings are dated 1886.

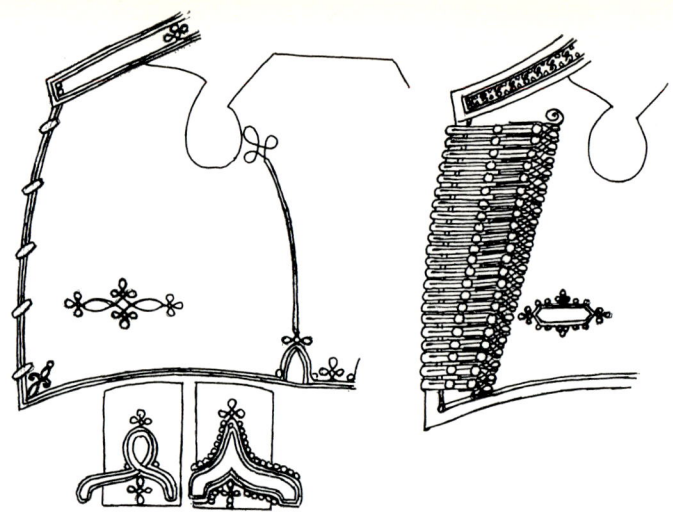

ABOVE: 18th Hussars. The stable jacket is all dark blue edged and traced with gold cord and tracing braid. An unusual feature is the way in which the back is cut square. The sleeve ornament on the left is for Captains and Lieutenants and is given as seven and a half inches high. The sleeve ornament on the right is for Field Officers and is marked eight and a half inches high. The vest is marked light blue but the actual colour was dark blue of a shade just lighter than the uniform colour. The lace on the collar and edges is gold while the decoration on the front is made up of gold chain gimp loops spaced threequarters of an inch apart and traced.

BELOW: The stable jacket of dark blue cloth is the same pattern for the 19th and 20th Hussars. Both were trimmed with gold lace and cords. The 20th Hussars drawing is dated 1892. The central diagram illustrates a mess vest of the 20th. It is marked crimson, edged with a pattern of eyes in gold tracing. The original sketch is dated 1883 and is marked as cancelled. The drawing for the third garment is marked 20th Hussars, 1891. Remarks on the sketch note that the fatigue jacket is blue serge with gold braid round collar, plain shoulder strap, black flat buttons on breast pockets, plain sleeves, no side pockets and four and a half inch slit up side seam. The jacket fastened with five brass olivets up the front. Field officers collars were decorated with a row of eyes on the front and top edge.

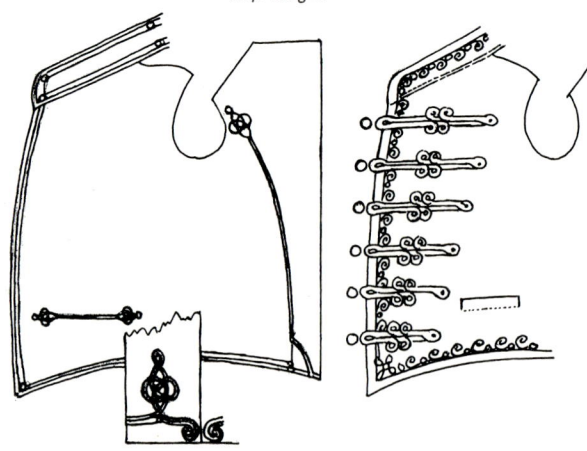

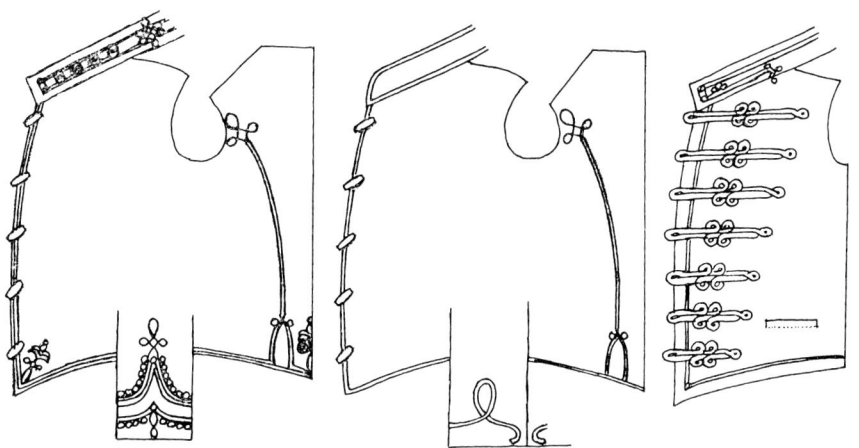

ABOVE: 15th Hussars. The stable jacket on the left is the pattern worn by Field Officers. The centre drawing shows the pattern worn by Captains and Lieutenants. The jacket was dark blue decorated with gold lace and tracing cord. The tailor's notes give the jacket as being lined scarlet, the Field Officer's sleeve ornament as being eight inches high, the lace on the cuff being one inch wide and the collar lace being three-quarters of an inch wide. The sleeve ornament for Captains and Lieutenants was given as five inches high. The vest is scarlet edged with gold lace and decorated with seven rows of gold chain gimp. The top row is marked as being five and a half inches long, the bottom row as three and a quarter inches long.

The officers of the 10th Hussars, 1898. The officers are all wearing the regimental pattern patrol jacket except for the 2nd Lieutenant standing to the left who is wearing a stable jacket. The round forage cap was dark blue with a band of 1¾ inch gold lace. On top of the cap was a gold purl button surrounded by a pattern of figured braid and a line of gold braid round the top seam.

The officers of the 14th Hussars, 1899. The uniform and equipment is that which the regiment wore at the commencement of the South African War. The colour of the uniform was a light shade of khaki. The leather equipment was brown and the haversack strap was khaki webbing. The revolver and ammunition pouch were placed on the waist belt, and a whistle can be seen on the left hand brace. The gaiters were of the Strohwesser pattern.

The officers of the 13th Hussars, 1898. Various orders of dress can be seen in this photograph, although all the officers are wearing the blue frock with one exception. The duty officers are wearing the blue and white folding field cap in Drill Order. With this the full dress pouch belt and a plain black sabretache are worn.

This Guard Room scene shows the dismounted Full Dress worn by other ranks. A corporal, trooper and sergeant are shown. The pattern of uniform was the same for all regiments. The interesting points to be noted in this picture are that where officers had olivet fasteners on the front of the tunic other ranks had ball buttons. The black pouch is carried on the white pouch belt and a long white sword knot can be seen on the sergeant's sword.

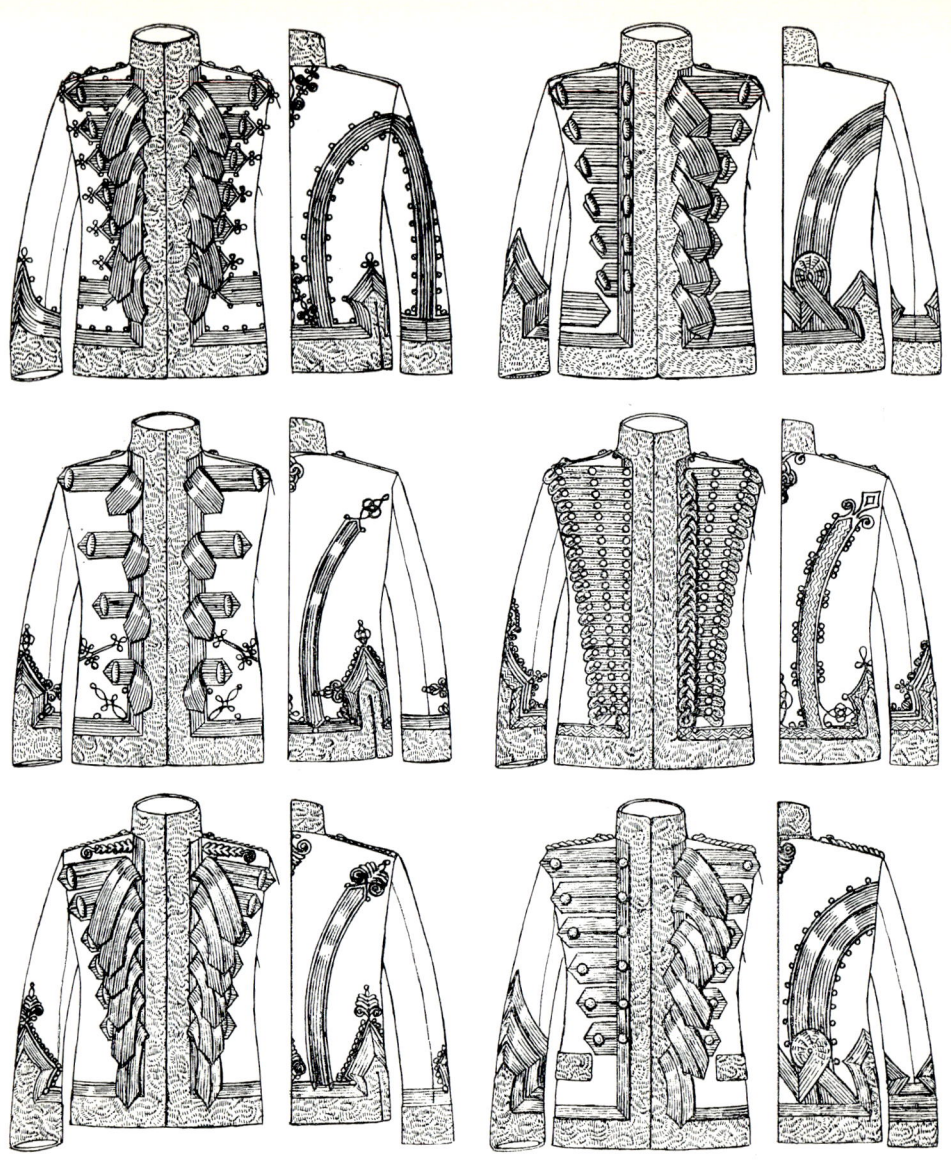

The last pattern of patrol jackets worn by officers of Hussar regiments. For all regiments the colours were the same, dark blue edged all round with black astrakhan, all braid and tracing cords being black mohair. Although very sombre in colours these jackets were very attractive and very fine examples of the military tailor's art. The last time that these jackets were described in Dress Regulations was in the edition of 1900, this in fact being the first illustrated edition. The only other illustrated editions were those of 1904 and 1911. For most regiments the patrol jackets were replaced in 1902 with the double breasted frock coat.

Top left: 3rd Hussars. Top right: 4th Hussars. Middle left: 7th Hussars. Middle right: 8th Hussars. Bottom left: 10th Hussars. Bottom right: 11th Hussars.

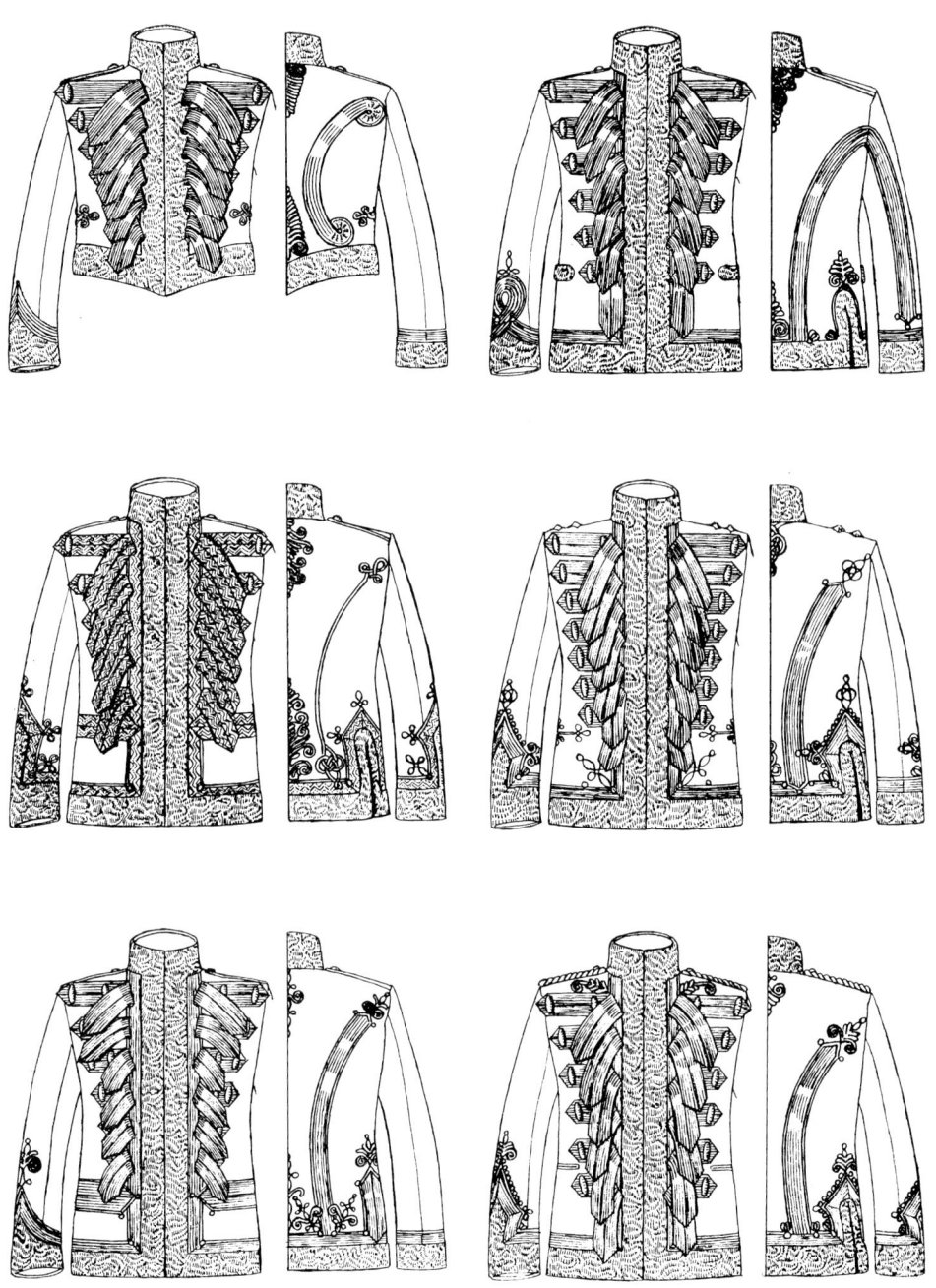

Top left: 13th Hussars. Top right: 14th Hussars. Middle left: 15th Hussars. Middle right: 18th Hussars. Bottom left: 19th Hussars. Bottom right: 20th Hussars.

Officers of the 13th Hussars, c. 1898, are shown wearing the patrol jacket and the serge jacket. The short patrol jacket was distinctive to the 13th Hussars. Further distinctions of the regiment were the buff collar on the blue frock (the colour buff was in fact white), the white stripes on the overalls, and a dark blue forage cap with a gold lace band and gold tracing on the crown. The 2nd Lieutenant and the Lieutenant sitting in the foreground can be identified by the fact that the 2nd Lieutenant has no rank insignia on the shoulder straps and the Lieutenant a single star. This was changed in 1904 when the insignia for a 2nd Lieutenant became one star and for Lieutenants two stars.

4: Officers' Full Dress Sabretaches

ALTHOUGH Dress Regulations for the Army were only published at irregular intervals those printed from 1822 to 1846 give a regulation size for sabretaches, this being fifteen inches in depth, nine inches across the top and thirteen inches across the bottom. From sabretaches still in existence it can be seen that regiments frequently ignored these regulations; one of the Waterloo period measures fifteen and a half inches deep by ten and a quarter at the top by thirteen inches across the bottom while one of the 1830 period measures thirteen inches in depth, seven and three quarters across the top and ten and a half across the bottom. It was not until 1900 that measurements were again given in Dress Regulations. These order for Hussar regiments twelve inches in depth, seven and three quarters across the top and ten and a half inches wide at the bottom. In the following descriptions where sizes are given they can only be taken as approximate because of the variations in manufacture.

3rd Hussars, 1861-1902

The officers' full dress sabretache from 1861 to 1902 was faced with scarlet cloth and edged with gold regimental lace which had a central stripe of scarlet. The design on the face consisted of the crown in gold embroidery, the cap of the crown being crimson velvet. The jewels were embroidered in silver, red, and green thread. Beneath the crown the cypher 'V.R.,' was embroidered in gold. Beneath the cypher was a garter of bright blue silk edged with gold, the garter bearing the motto 'Honi soit qui mal y pense'. Inside the garter on a scarlet ground was the White Horse of Hanover in silver. Beneath the garter also, in bright blue silk edged gold, was a scroll bearing the words 'Nec Aspera Terrent'. Surrounding the garter and motto scrolls were sprays of laurel embroidered gold on which were scrolls bearing eleven battle honours, all scrolls being

Top left: 3rd Hussars Officers sabretache 1861-1902
Top right: 4th Hussars Officers sabretache 1861-1902
Bottom left: 7th Hussars Officers sabretache 1820-1902
Bottom right: 8th Hussars Officers sabretache 1881-1902
A full description of these sabretaches is given in the text.

of bright blue silk edged and lettered gold. This sabretache measured twelve and a quarter inches deep by nine inches across the top and eleven and a half across the bottom.

4th Hussars, 1861-1902

The full dress sabretache was of scarlet leather faced with scarlet cloth and edged round the sides and bottom with gold regimental lace which had a central stripe of crimson. The crown was embroidered in gold and had a cap of crimson velvet. The jewels were embroidered in silver, red

Top left: 10th Hussars Officers sabretache 1880-1902
Top right: 11th Hussars Officers sabretache 1859-1902
Bottom left: 13th Hussars Officers sabretache 1861-1902
Bottom right: 14th Hussars Officers sabretache 1861-1902
A full description of these sabretaches is given in the text.

and green threads. Below the crown was the cypher 'V.R.' in gold. Below the cypher was '4' above 'H' in gold surrounded by laurel leaves bearing scrolls containing regimental battle honours. The scrolls were dark blue velvet edged and lettered in gold. The laurel leaves were also embroidered in gold. Measurements are twelve inches deep, eight inches across the top and ten and three quarter inches across the bottom.

7th Hussars, 1807-1902

On conversion to Hussars the first sabretache is shown in illustrations to be faced with white cloth edged all round with gold lace and bearing

69

Top left: 15th Hussars Officers sabretache 1830-1880
Top right: 18th Hussars Officers sabretache 1883?-1902
Bottom left: 19th Hussars Officers sabretache 1861-1902
Bottom right: 20th Hussars Officers sabretache 1885-1902
A full description of these sabretaches is given in the text.

on the face a crown in full colours above the Queen's Cypher 'C.R.,' in gold. A change in colour appears to have come about in 1812 when the face was changed to scarlet, this remaining the colour until 1902. From 1812 the design was a gold crown embroidered in full colour above the monogram 'G.R.' in gold. A feature of the 7th Hussars sabretache was that at no time did it carry sprays of laurel or battle honour scrolls. From 1820 to 1902 the only design on the face was the crown embroidered in full colours above the regimental cypher 'Q.O.'. The 7th Hussar sabretaches were always edged with gold lace. Measurements were thirteen inches deep by eight and a half across the top and twelve inches across the bottom.

8th Hussars, 1822-1902

Drawings and photographs illustrate four different designs for the period that the 8th wore the sabretache with Hussar clothing up to 1902. The basic design was the same, the alterations being when extra honour scrolls were added. All patterns bore the crown embroidered in full colours above the 'V.R.' cypher. The cypher was unusual in that it was embroidered in silver. Superimposed on the cypher was the Royal Arms, a Lion standing on a crown all in coloured embroidery, the cap of the gold crown being of crimson velvet. What appears to be the first pattern is faced with scarlet cloth edged all round with gold lace similar to the Royal Artillery pattern. Beneath the crown of the Royal Arms the Roman numeral 'VIII' in displayed gold. Beneath this is the Irish Harp in gold with strings embroidered silver, and with each side of the Harp a spray of shamrock in silver and two scrolls in gold silk thread, one bearing the words 'The King's Royal' and the second having the words 'Irish Hussars'.

The measurements were thirteen inches deep by eight and a half across the top and eleven inches across the bottom. This pattern is most probably that of 1820 as it does not carry the regimental motto or the battle honours 'Hindoostan' and 'Leswarree' which were authorised to be borne by the regiment on March 14, 1825. The regiment was also authorised to retain the motto 'Pristinæ virtutis memores' on the same date. The next pattern bears the same central badges, the crown, cypher, superimposed Royal Arms, numeral and harp, but between the top crown and royal cypher there is a scroll bearing the words 'The King's Royal Irish Hussars' and on each side of the harp, placed on the shamrock, are two scrolls. These four scrolls carry the honours awarded to the regiment for service in the Crimean War. This sabretache was edged on the two sides and bottom with a narrow gold lace of regimental pattern which was woven to represent the shamrock. The next pattern which must be of the same period, shortly after 1855, was very similar but slightly larger, with a wider regimental pattern shamrock. Gold lace edged the two sides and bottom, while the scroll below the crown now carried the regimental motto. Beneath the harp was a scroll for 'Central India' and placed on the sprays of shamrock each side of the harp were three battle honour scrolls. Measurements were thirteen and a half deep, eight and a half wide at the top and ten and a quarter inches across the bottom. The last design carried eight battle honour scrolls, four on each side of the harp. This pattern was the last to be worn in the regiment, it would be dated after 1880 as it carries the 'Afghanistan' honour.

10th Hussars

The first pattern is shown in contemporary paintings and was made from crimson leather, faced with scarlet cloth which was embroidered with the Prince of Wales's Plumes and motto scrolls. Below the plumes was a crown above the cypher 'G.R.'. The edges were silver laced. The plumes and motto of the Prince of Wales have always appeared on the face of the sabretaches of the 10th Hussars and from 1810 to 1902 the lace on

71

the edges was gold.

From 1820 to 1830 the design was a crown in full colours placed on the plumes with a motto scroll each side. Below this was the doubled and reversed cypher 'G.R.', in silver embroidery, the numeral 'X' in gold, and at the bottom two blue scrolls edged gold bearing the honours 'Peninsula' and 'Waterloo'. The scrolls were surrounded with sprays of silver laurel leaves. This was edged on three sides with gold lace. Measurements were thirteen inches deep, eight across the top and eleven inches across the bottom. This pattern appears to have remained in use until 1879, the only alterations being when the Royal Cyphers were changed. The final pattern abolished in 1902 was edged on three sides with gold lace and bore the crown and Prince of Wales's Plumes and motto above the cypher 'V.R.', which was embroidered in gold. The numeral 'X' also gold and five honour scrolls which were dark blue, bordered and lettered gold and surrounded by sprays of gold laurel leaves. Measurements were twelve and a half inches deep, eight across the top and eleven and a half across the bottom.

11th Hussars

From 1840 to 1902 there were two designs both of crimson leather faced with crimson cloth. The first pattern was in use from 1840 to 1858 and the design on the face had a gold crown with a green orb and jewels embroidered in silver, red and green silks. Beneath the crown was a scroll bearing the words 'Prince Albert's Own Hussars'. Below this scroll was the doubled and reversed cypher 'V.R.'. Below the cypher were three scrolls with the honours 'Peninsula' 'Salamanca' and 'Waterloo'. Beneath the Salamanca scroll was a silver metal badge of 'The Sphinx'. The scrolls were made of purple velvet bordered and lettered in gold and were surrounded by sprays of laurel leaves also embroidered gold. The sides and bottom were edged with two inch gold lace of regimental pattern and across the top was a line of double plait gold embroidery and a line of gold chain gimp. The measurements were thirteen and a half inches deep, ten inches across the top and eleven and a half across the bottom. The colours for the second design carried from 1859 to 1902 were the same as for the first, the difference being that the crest of the Prince Consort was placed on the centre of the 'V.R.', cypher. This crest was the Arms of Saxony and consisted of a column of black and gold bands with a diagonal green band. Surmounting the pillars were yellow peacock's feathers, the eyes being embroidered in black, light blue, and green silk. Beneath the pillar was the motto 'Treu und fest' on a crimson velvet scroll. Surrounding the silver Sphinx badge were added four more honour scrolls for 'Alma', 'Inkerman', 'Balaclava', and 'Sevastopol', the scrolls being of purple velvet.

13th Hussars, 1861-1902

This sabretache measured twelve inches deep by eight inches across the top and ten and a half across the bottom. It was faced with white cloth bordered on three sides with one and three quarter inch wide regimental pattern gold lace. This lace had a central stripe of white (although the regulations always give the facing colour for the 13th Hussars as buff it was in fact white). The design on the face consisted of a crown embroidered in gold with a green orb and jewels in silver, red

The Maxim Gun detachment of the 13th Hussars, 1898. This interesting picture shows what appears to be an adaptation of a Royal Artillery gun carriage and limber. The harness is of the Artillery pattern. The gun team is in charge of the mounted sergeant. The men are all wearing the blue and white folding field cap and the dark blue frock with a white patch on the collar. Standing in front are a Staff Sergeant Drill Instructor and an officer wearing a patrol jacket.

and green. The cypher 'V.R.', was gold as were the laurel leaves. The regimental number was surrounded by a circle of light blue silk which bore the motto 'Viret in Æternum'. The six honour scrolls were also light blue, bordered and lettered gold.

14th Hussars, 1861-1902

Made of buff leather, this sabretache was faced with scarlet cloth, edged on three sides with two inch gold lace of regimental pattern. Across the top was a line of double plait gold embroidery and a line of gold chain gimp lace. The design on the face was the crown embroidered in full colours above the cypher 'V.R.'. Below the cypher was a Prussian Eagle all embroidered gold. Surrounding the eagle were sprays of gold laurel leaves and blue silk scrolls bearing the regimental battle honours. The scrolls were bordered and lettered gold. The approximate size was thirteen inches deep by eight inches across the top and eleven and a half across the bottom.

15th Hussars, 1807-1902

From 1807 to 1902 the sabretaches of the 15th were faced with scarlet. They were laced with silver from 1807 to 1819 and from 1826 to 1830. They were gold laced from 1820 to 1826 and from 1830 to 1902. The first pattern had the Imperial crown embroidered in gold and coloured silks. Below the crown, embroidered in silver, was a doubled and reversed 'G.R.' cypher. There were two silver scrolls lettered in gold,

An experimental gun carriage of the 14th Hussars, 1897. Adapted from the Royal Artillery gun carriage and limber the idea behind this experiment was for the regiment to provide its own fast moving fire support. Like the Maxim Gun detachment of the 13th, the horses appear to be equipped with Royal Artillery pattern harness.

one above the crown inscribed 'Merebimur' and one below the cypher bearing the honour 'Emsdorf'. This sabretache was edged all round with a special pattern of silver lace. The next pattern had a different type of lace which had a thick wave pattern. The design on the face was gold embroidered, featuring a crown with the honour scroll 'Peninsula' above. Below the crown were two scrolls bearing the honours 'Emsdorf' and 'Villiers-en-Couche'. Below this was the doubled cypher 'G.R.', with the honour scroll for Waterloo below the cypher.

From 1830 the very elaborate design in the centre first appeared, this being continued until 1902. The central device consisted of a gold crown embroidered in full colours. Standing on the crown was a gold lion, the crown and lion being surrounded by a trophy of arms and standards all gold except for the silver to represent pike heads, sword blades and bayonets. Above the trophy of arms was a crown with two gold scrolls beneath bearing the honours 'EMSDORF' and 'VILLIERS-EN-COUCHE'. Below the trophy of arms were five honour scrolls and sprays of laurel, all gold. An alteration was made after 1880 when the additional honour 'Afghanistan' was placed beneath the 'Waterloo' scroll.

18th Hussars, 1807-1821

A painting of an officer shortly before the regiment was disbanded shows the sabretache of the first regiment of 18th Hussars to have been faced with bright blue cloth edged all round with silver lace, the device on the front was a gold crown above the cypher 'G.R.', with an ornamental figuring around the base and sides of the cypher.

18th Hussars, 1858-1902

There were two patterns both faced with scarlet cloth, the design on the face being a gold crown in full colours over the cypher 'V.R.'. Below

74

the cypher was '18' over 'H' with sprays of laurel leaves each side, all embroidered in gold. One pattern has scrolls for 'Peninsula' and 'Waterloo' and beneath these the motto 'Pro Rege, pro Lege, pro Patria conamur'. All scrolls were dark blue. This pattern is edged all round with gold lace and is believed to be the first pattern, as a contemporary print indicates this design although the motto was not officially authorised until 1883. The measurements were fourteen and a half inches deep, nine across the top and twelve inches across the bottom. The second measures thirteen inches by eight and a half by twelve and is edged on three sides only with gold lace. On the face only the 'Peninsula' and 'Waterloo' scrolls are shown. A note in an article on this sabretache states this to be the last pattern although the date of the change is not given.

19th Hussars, 1861-1902

This sabretache was faced with scarlet cloth and was edged on three sides with regimental lace which had a central stripe of white. The design on the face was made up of the 'V.R.' cypher in gold with a gold crown above, the crown having a crimson velvet cap and jewels worked in silver red and green thread. Below the cypher was a silver elephant with above and below blue velvet scrolls edged gold bearing, above the honour 'Assaye' and below 'Niagara', a sprig of laurel in gold each side of the elephant.

20th Hussars, 1861-1902

The 20th had a crimson faced sabretache from 1861 to 1902. Although the basic design remained the same a slight change was made in 1885. The design on the face was a crown in gold with a crimson velvet cap and jewels worked in silver, red and green. Below this was the 'V.R.' cypher in gold. Below the cypher was a gold ring enclosing '20H' on a crimson ground, and each side of the ring were sprays of laurels all embroidered gold. The battle honour 'Peninsula' was on a blue velvet gold edged scroll below the regimental number. The change in 1885 was made to fit in the honour 'Suakin 1884'. The 'Peninsula' scroll being placed to the left, the 'Suakin, 1884' to the right. The lace edging on three sides had a central line of crimson.

21st Hussars, 1861-1897

From 1861 to 1864 the sabretache was faced with scarlet cloth and from 1864 to 1897 with cloth of French grey colour. The actual design on the face remained the same for both patterns being a gold crown with coloured embroidery to represent the jewels. The cypher 'V.R.', was carried, plus sprays of laurel and a ring enclosing '21' over 'H' on a ground of the facing colour, all embroidered in gold. This was edged on both sides and bottom with gold regimental lace which had a central stripe of white on the scarlet pattern and a central line of French grey on the 1864, 1897 pattern.

Mounted trooper in review order 1895